EXECUTIVE FUNCTION: FOUNDATIONS FOR LEARNING AND TEACHING

Patricia W. Newhall

LANDMARK SCHOOL OUTREACH PROGRAM

PROFESSIONAL DEVELOPMENT FOR EDUCATORS

The information and educational interventions presented in this book are for classroom use and should not be construed as substitutions or replacements for evaluations and recommendations from physicians, psychologists, or neuropsychologists.

Individuals pictured in this book bear no relation to examples or profiles in this book.

Copyright © 2014 Landmark School Outreach Program
PO Box 227
Prides Crossing, MA 01965
landmarkoutreach.org

ISBN 978-0-9713297-5-1

Printed in the United States of America.

To reference this text, please use the following citation:
Newhall, P. W. (2014). *Executive function: Foundations for learning and teaching.* In P. W. Newhall (Ed.), *Language-based teaching series.* Prides Crossing, MA: Landmark School Outreach Program.

Contents

Materials for Reproduction

Online Resource Available

The resources in the What to Do sections at the end of each chapter may be photocopied from this book for personal or classroom use. They are also available online for printing or customizing at www.landmarkoutreach.org/ef-resources. When you open this page, enter the username **(foundations)** and the password **(OUTREACH)**.

About Us
Landmark School
Outreach Program

Established in 1977 as the professional development arm of Landmark School, Landmark Outreach's mission is to empower students through their teachers. Landmark Outreach serves both general and special education professionals, with the goal of sharing knowledge and strategies that contribute to students' classroom success. Landmark Outreach provides language-based consulting and program design in collaboration with schools and districts, summer Professional Development Institutes, online professional development courses, and publications. Information about Landmark Outreach's programs and publications is available at landmarkoutreach.org.

Founded in 1971, Landmark School is recognized internationally as a leader in the field of language-based learning disabilities. A coeducational boarding and day school for elementary, middle, and high school students, Landmark individualizes instruction for each student and emphasizes the development of language and learning skills within a highly structured living and learning environment. Information about Landmark School is available online at landmarkschool.org.

Introduction
Language-Based Teaching Series

As educators, we are deeply invested in helping young people reach their potential. The curricula we design and the instruction we deliver are informed by our goal of fostering students' development into individuals who are intellectually engaged in the world of ideas, active in their communities, morally and spiritually aware, and physically healthy. We coach our students to become independent thinkers and creative problem-solvers and decision-makers who communicate effectively and act with responsible purpose. Often, though, our lofty goals are obscured by the daily grind of lesson planning, grading, advising, coaching, and the myriad other responsibilities teachers commonly shoulder.

Landmark Outreach's *Language-Based Teaching Series* is about empowering students to reach their academic potential. Young people arrive in our classrooms with biological makeups and life experiences that influence both what and how they learn. Some students have learning disabilities; some do not. All students have potential, and all students need our help to reach it.

As it takes a village to raise a child, it takes a school to train a scholar. We all—faculty, staff, and administrators—are responsible for facilitating each student's educational rearing. Sometimes, in our urgency to ready students for the competitive adult world, we forget that we are teaching young people who need models, explicit instruction, and guided practice in order to gain independence. As one school's principal commented, "Too frequently, we lose sight of the student for the assignment."

Some students come to us with a full complement of academic skills and enthusiasm for schoolwork. We praise the quality of their independent work, and in our own minds hold them up as the standard by which we judge other students. Many students fall short, and we wonder why. Our wondering leads us to all sorts of assumptions.

The *Language-Based Teaching Series* offers information and practical resources to help teachers and administrators understand and support the students who fall short of expectations. From a synthesis of research on learning to insights gained in the class-room, the series aims to support educators' efforts to help all students learn effectively. Each book focuses on one topic, organizes chapters around *what to know* and *what to do*, and provides strategies, checklists, questionnaires, and other tools that can be reproduced as-is or accessed online and customized. These materials are intended to spark ideas and help with understanding students' thinking, scaffolding learning, and implementing skills-based instruction.

Of course, there are no quick fixes for students with learning difficulties, and no single book or program can address all learners' needs. This series aims to get teachers thinking broadly about students' strengths and vulnerabilities, how they learn, and what helps them gain essential skills.

Landmark Outreach encourages readers of our publications to contact us with questions, comments, and ideas. Each of our books has a dedicated feedback page on our website. Please consider posting your thoughts about what you've read! To learn when new books in the series are released, visit landmarkoutreach.org and join the Landmark Outreach mailing list.

Landmark's Six Teaching Principles™

At the heart of Landmark's instructional strategies and programs are six teaching principles.

PROVIDE OPPORTUNITIES FOR SUCCESS

Providing students with opportunities for success is key. Failure and poor self-esteem often result when teachers challenge students beyond their ability. Landmark begins teaching students at their current level of ability. This approach improves basic skills and enhances confidence. As Landmark teachers introduce each new skill, they provide basic examples and assignments to build confidence and keep students from becoming overwhelmed. As the information becomes more challenging, teachers assign students easier problems to supplement the more difficult ones. In this way, those students who are having trouble with the material complete at least part of the assignment while they work at understanding and learning to apply new information. Teachers give themselves permission to provide students with whatever structure is necessary to help students be successful, such as study guides for tests, templates for writing, and guidelines for projects. Only with a solid foundation of basic skills and confidence can students make progress.

USE MULTISENSORY APPROACHES

Multisensory teaching is effective for all students. In general, it means presenting all information to students via three sensory modalities: visual, auditory, and tactile. Visual presentation techniques include graphic organizers for structuring writing and pictures for reinforcing instruction; auditory presentation techniques include conducting thorough discussions and reading aloud; tactile presentation techniques include manipulating blocks and creating paragraphs about objects students can hold in their hands. Overall, implementing a multisensory approach to teaching is not difficult; in fact, many teachers use such an approach. It is important, however, to be aware of the three sensory modes and to plan to integrate them every day.

MICRO-UNIT AND STRUCTURE TASKS

Effective teaching involves breaking information down into its smallest units and providing clear guidelines for all assignments. This is especially important for students with learning disabilities. "Micro-uniting" and structuring are elements of directive teaching, which Landmark consistently uses with students. Micro-uniting means analyzing the parts of a task or assignment and teaching those parts one step at a time. Teachers organize information so students can see and follow the steps clearly and sequentially. As students learn to micro-unit for themselves, they become less likely to give up on tasks that appear confusing or overwhelming. Consequently, these strategies enable students to proceed in a step-by-step, success-oriented way.

ENSURE AUTOMATIZATION THROUGH PRACTICE AND REVIEW

Automatization is the process of learning and assimilating a task or skill so completely that it can be consistently completed with little or no conscious attention. Repetition and review (spiraling) are critical. Sometimes, students appear to understand a concept, only to forget it a day, week, or month later. It is not until students have automatized a skill that they can effectively remember and use it as a foundation for new tasks. Teachers must therefore provide ample opportunities for students to repeat and review learned material. For example, the Landmark writing process emphasizes practice and consistency. Students always brainstorm, map/outline, draft, and proofread in the same way. This provides them with an ongoing, consistent review of learned skills.

PROVIDE MODELS

Providing models is simple, yet very important. It is one of the most effective teaching techniques. Models are concrete examples of what teachers expect. This does not mean that teachers are doing assignments for students. Models are standards to which students can compare their own work. A model or example of a completed assignment serves as a springboard for students to begin the assignment. For example, teachers should give students a model of a sequential paragraph when teaching basic sequential paragraph writing.

INCLUDE STUDENTS IN THE LEARNING PROCESS

Students are not passive receptacles to fill with information. They come to class with their own frames of reference. Their unique experiences and knowledge affect them as learners and should be taken into account. Therefore, during every exercise, teachers should accept student input as much as possible. They should justify assignments, accept suggestions, solicit ideas, and provide ample time for students to share ideas. Teachers should include students in assessing their own progress by reviewing test results, written reports, and educational plans. Creating and improvising opportunities to involve students in the learning process allows students to become aware of how they learn and why certain skills benefit them. As a result, students are motivated and more likely to apply those skills when working independently. In short, an included student becomes an invested student who is eager to learn.

Chapter 1
Executive Function

WHAT TO KNOW

As educators, we want to inspire and empower students to
become creative and independent thinkers. At the very least, we
want to provide curriculum and instruction that develop students'
language and literacy skills, learning and study skills, and self-
efficacy. These three areas develop interactively and dynamically
to create academic proficiency. They are rooted in cognitive and
psychological processes that are coordinated by executive function. Figure 1 illustrates these relationships.

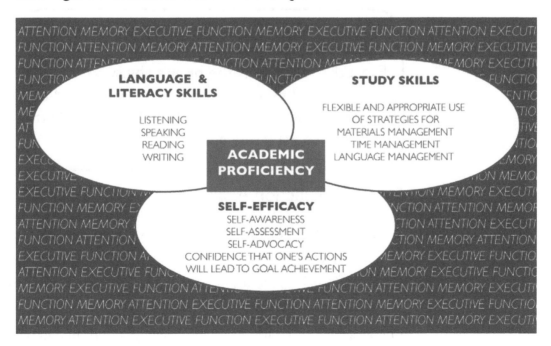

Figure 1. Elements of academic proficiency

> Executive function is the foundation for academic proficiency because it describes our ability to engage in goal-oriented behavior that culminates in a product or achievement.

Executive function is the foundation for academic proficiency because it describes our ability to engage in goal-oriented behavior that culminates in a product or achievement. Such behavior includes setting goals, creating and following plans to achieve them, self-evaluating progress toward them, and shifting attitudes and behaviors as needed in order to meet the goal. Disruptions in one or more of the cognitive and psychological processes coordinated by executive function, or with the coordination itself, can lead to difficulties in school. Difficulties may result when a student faces challenges with processing information (learning), demonstrating learning (production), or some combination of the two.

Our understanding of the brain has increased tremendously since the advent of positron emission tomography (PET scans) and functional magnetic resonance imaging (fMRI), which show the brain at work. Though researchers have made great strides in understanding how the brain processes language, they continue to investigate why some individuals learn more efficiently and effectively than others. Of interest to researchers are the relationships between school performance and executive function, attention, memory, emotion, and effort, which are but some of the many cognitive and psychological processes essential to learning.

EXECUTIVE FUNCTION

Executive function is the brain's ability to coordinate the cognitive and psychological processes needed to initiate, sustain, monitor and adapt the behaviors and attitudes required to achieve a goal.

Executive Function Analogy

Researchers from various disciplines have posed different theories and models of executive function, yet all generally agree that the term describes the brain's skill at accessing and coordinating all of its processes toward goal-oriented behavior. Such behavior is, of course, essential to individuals' success both in and out of school. Brown's (2007) analogy of the brain as a symphony and executive function as its conductor states it clearly:

> *Regardless of their expertise, the musicians need a competent conductor who will select the piece to play, make sure they start playing at the same time and stay on tempo, fade in the strings and then bring in the brass, and manage them as they interpret the music. Without an effective conductor, the symphony will not produce good music. (p. 23)*

The quality of the orchestra's production depends in part upon the skill of its individual musicians. If the strings section is out of tune or plays poorly, the music will suffer. Even when each musician is in tune and playing well, coordinating all of the musicians to produce beautiful music requires another layer of expertise, which comes from the conductor.

According to Brown, "Until we know much more about underlying neural processes, any descriptive model [of executive function] is likely to be a bit arbitrary" (2005, p. 21). While many researchers offer descriptions of executive function (Anderson, Jacobs, & Anderson, 2008; Barkley, 1997, 2012; Dawson & Guare, 2010; McCloskey, Perkins, & Van Divner, 2009; Meltzer, 2010), Brown's model (2007) is straightforward in describing six clusters that operate in an integrated way. These are illustrated in figure 2.

> Disruptions in one or more of the cognitive and psychological processes coordinated by executive function, or with the coordination itself, can lead to difficulties in school.

Executive Function and Academic Skills

A student with weaknesses in one or more underlying skill areas of academic proficiency—difficulty managing language, for example—may exhibit weaknesses within Brown's six clusters because of the underlying deficit. Students who have difficulty reading dedicate so many cognitive and psychological resources to decoding and making sense of individual words on the page that they may avoid the activity entirely or appear to lack focus, effort, emotional control, or the ability to self-monitor. Their executive function is overwhelmed and unable to manage the task because they lack the skills to achieve the goal. Some neuropsychologists

EXECUTIVE FUNCTION CLUSTERS

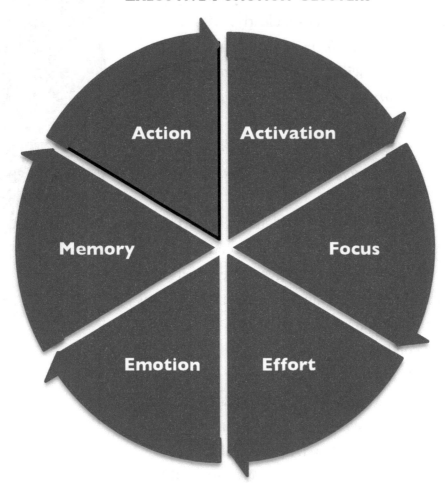

Figure 2. Executive function clusters (text from Brown, 2007. p. 24).

informally call this phenomenon "bottom-up difficulties" with executive function because a specific underlying skill deficit interferes with overall executive function.

Other students have "top-down difficulties." They perform poorly in school because of weak executive function. While they may not have the auditory or visual processing deficits that cause reading problems, their decoding and comprehension skills may be poor because they struggle to activate, focus, sustain effort and speed, access and use memory, and apply strategies flexibly toward achieving the goal of reading fluently. Effective school learning and performance require accessing, monitoring, regulating, and synchronizing all the clusters of executive function.

Whether they are "bottom-up" or "top-down," executive function difficulties can interfere with success at one or more points, as figure 3 shows. To succeed at any given task, students must know what to do, how to do it, begin and work through each step of a task, adjust to challenges, and execute the task. It is important for students and their teachers to identify where the difficulty lies so that interventions can be targeted effectively. Reflection on the process of learning and demonstration of learning is also an essential approach to building executive skill. When students can identify what strategies helped them succeed in the task completion process, they can use these same strategies to build future success. This type of targeted reflection builds students' self-efficacy because they learn how their actions relate to their performance.

Teachers cannot "cure" students with impairments in executive function or the processes it coordinates. We *can* provide scaffolded instruction of strategies that support skill development so students can manage the complex curricular demands placed on them.

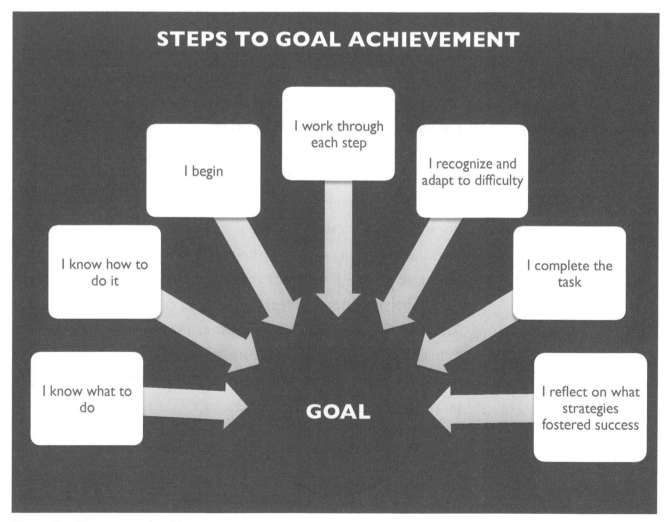

Figure 3. Steps to goal achievement.

> Many internal and external factors can interfere with executive function and, therefore, effective learning and goal-directed behavior.

Development of Executive Function

Executive function begins developing in infancy and continues through late adolescence (mid-twenties). As an individual matures, Russel A. Barkley describes eight inter-related developmental capacities that arise from the integrated maturation of the pre-frontal cortex and executive function. These eight capacities are spatial capacity, temporal capacity, motivational capacity, inhibitory capacity, conceptual/abstract capacity, behavioral-structural capacity, social capacity, and cultural capacity (2012, pp. 68-71). As the pre-frontal cortex and executive function mature, executive function begins to drive outward to coordinate all activity from the personal, social, community and cultural arenas (2012, p. 68).

Interferences with Executive Function

Many internal and external factors can interfere with executive function and, therefore, effective learning and goal-directed behavior. While short-term interferences are quite common for most people, longer-term or more severe interferences are cause for concern and appropriate intervention.

Short-term interferences commonly occur due to physical illness or injury, or to stress reactions to external occurrences. For example, when a person is running a fever or feeling nauseated, the "to do list" often does not get made or done, and even the thought of learning something new or complex can seem overwhelming. When we don't feel well, our goal-oriented behavior is directed toward helping ourselves feel better so we can resume our regular activities. Similarly, emotional stress can interfere with our ability to make or carry out plans or learn effectively. Resolving the stressful situation or seeking support to help calm ourselves takes precedent over our usual activities.

Some internal and external interferences can cause long-term or more severe interferences with executive function. A variety of physical illnesses, injuries, and disorders can disrupt the development of or the effective engagement of executive function. Some individuals with multiple sclerosis for example, experience not only physical symptoms of the disease, but also have difficulty coordinating and regulating themselves in order to achieve a goal. Traumatic brain injuries interfere with the development of executive function if the injury occurs during childhood or adolescence, and can cause profound changes in functioning for affected adults. In addition, stress—particularly traumatic stress or long-term stress—can impede executive function. Individuals who suffer from anxiety disorders, depression, developmental trauma, and post-traumatic stress disorder commonly exhibit weak executive functioning. It is also important to be aware that children living in stressful environments often have difficulty with the self-regulation that robust executive function coordinates. Children at risk for interferences with the development of executive function include those who are exposed to physical or emotional violence, those who live with substance abusers, those who live with caregivers who cannot nurture them physically and/or emotionally, and those who experience interruptions in safe and secure living situations.

> Difficulties with executive function vary dramatically in relation to the environmental context and the severity of interference with goal orientation and achievement. A student may have no difficulty in one class or activity but profound trouble managing others.

Knowing When to Intervene

Knowing when intervention is called for, and what interventions to provide can be extremely challenging and frustrating for educators and caregivers, even when they know quite a lot about executive function. Difficulties with executive function vary dramatically in relation to the environmental context and the severity of interference with goal-oriented behavior. A student may have no difficulty in one class or activity but profound trouble managing others. A student may exhibit no executive function difficulty in elementary school, but start to struggle in middle school, or high school, or college. Figure 4 offers a graphic with questions to consider when reflecting on students' academic and interpersonal behavior.

One aim of this book is to provide readers with information to assist in thinking and observing various aspects of executive function interference. Many students have significant weaknesses in this area that go unrecognized. Some struggle with executive function enough to cause anxiety and impede their performance, but not enough that educators or caregivers recognize a problem. Others exhibit noticeable difficulties with schoolwork and/or have identified behavioral issues that stem from disorders of attention or executive function, but they are misdiagnosed or underdiagnosed. Formal assessments of executive function are notoriously unreliable because the assessments usually occur in an environment that is quite different from the student's functional living and learning environments.

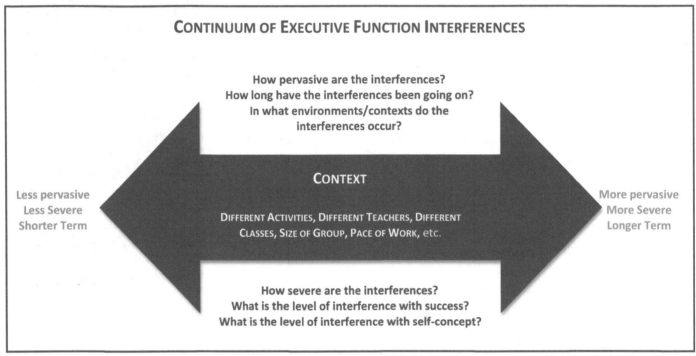

Figure 4. Continuum of executive function interferences.

Interventions for Executive Function

No single book or workshop could provide a thorough course of intervention for difficulties with executive function. The role executive function plays in learning and living is so complex that a one-size-fits-all answer to the question, "What should I do to build my students' (or my own) skills?" would be doomed to fail. Yet, there are principles that can guide us to empower ourselves as teachers and our students as learners.

One of the most important principles is to acknowledge and remember that all learners, including ourselves, are unique. Our individual responses to opportunities for learning and demonstrating our proficiency vary according to our past experiences, the contexts in which we live and learn in the present, and our goals.

It is essential to become aware of our own learning and teaching profiles as well as our students' learning and performance profiles. How? We must be guided by a second important principle: we educators are learners ourselves. Not only do we learn from our colleagues, books, and professional development activities, we also learn from our students. As we strive to become ever-better listeners, observers, and communicators with our colleagues AND our students about what works and what doesn't in the dynamic ecosystem of the classroom, we become more attuned teachers. When we are attuned, we experience continual growth in our understanding of how people learn and demonstrate their learning most successfully, and what we can do to empower our students.

What You'll Find in This Book

Chapters 1-4 in this book offer a synthesis of information about an aspect of executive function, a selection of student profiles with reflective questions for educators, comments from students about their learning experiences, and models of suggested teaching approaches and strategies.

Chapter 1 introduces executive function as a construct for understanding the process that drives human beings' goal-oriented behavior. Chapter 2 describes the roles attention and memory play in the learning process and the workings of executive function. Chapter 3 extends the description of attention and memory by exploring the influences emotion, motivation, and effort have on learning and behavior. Chapter 4 explores the role executive function plays in the development of academic proficiency.

Chapter 5 builds upon the previous chapters' acknowledgement that successful learning and performance is dependent upon context and unique to each individual. The chapter offers a way to think and talk about our own and our students' learning styles, differences, and disabilities.

> We educators are learners ourselves. Not only do we learn from our colleagues, books, and professional development activities, we also learn from our students. As we strive to become ever-better listeners, observers, and communicators with our colleagues AND our students about what works and what doesn't in the dynamic ecosystem of the classroom, we become more attuned teachers.

STUDENT PROFILES

Student Profiles

The student profiles section of each chapter introduces different executive function facets of five students: Enrique, Petra, Adonis, Jonelsi, and Nathan. Each experiences difficulties in school that teachers must recognize, analyze and address. The profiles are composites of several actual students whose names have been changed.

Students have unique learning profiles that reflect their educational experience from the past and influence their current experience in school. Elements of their profiles include their learning, thinking, and personality styles; their emotion, motivation, and effort; and their particular areas of need for language acquisition and use. All students who struggle in school—particularly those with a learning disability—benefit from structured, multisensory, language-based skills instruction as well as opportunities to succeed. The student profiles in this book are included to encourage educators' thinking about and planning for the success of the students in their classes.

Consider Student Background and Current Performance

As you read about each student's background and current performance, keep in mind the following questions:

Why might this student be struggling?

What is preventing this student from achieving success?

What steps would I take to support this student?

Also think about your own students:

Who among my students is not meeting expectations?

What clues do I have about why they are not succeeding?

What steps have I taken to support these students?

What should my next steps be?

ENRIQUE is an 8-year old boy who attends his neighborhood elementary school. Diagnosed with dyslexia/reading disorder in second grade, he receives special education services in a 2x per cycle program run by a reading specialist. He also receives 2x per cycle speech-language services for articulation. Over the 10 months since he has received reading instruction, he has gained one grade level in skill (from <K to 1st grade level). Enrique has many friends at school, and is a natural athlete who enjoys playing town soccer, basketball, and baseball. He says recess is his favorite subject. At home, his mother says he is highly active, playing with friends and riding his bike. It is difficult for her to get him to settle down to do his homework, and he becomes very tired when the work involves any reading, writing, or math. When required to do homework, he becomes very angry and cries. His teachers have also noted that he "lacks the stamina" to keep at these activities until his work is completed, but he does not display the emotional outbursts his mother describes. Enrique is achieving significantly below his peers, and his parents and teachers are trying to figure out what else to do to support his learning.

PETRA is an 11-year old girl who attends an urban charter school. According to her teachers, she is very serious and works hard, but she does not achieve at the same level as most of her peers. They have encouraged Petra to seek them out for extra help and to ask questions when she doesn't understand something, or the work is too difficult, but Petra does not do this. Often, she sits in front of her books doing nothing until a teacher approaches her. Her homework completion is inconsistent, and she often comes to school without the things she needs for the day. Petra's father says she is quiet at home and helps out a great deal with housework and taking care of her three younger brothers. She does not appear to have friends, although she often participates in recess games with other girls.

ADONIS is a 13-year old boy who attends his city's public middle school. When it comes to speaking, Adonis is confident and persuasive, but both his reading and writing skills fall significantly below grade level. When he was in 6th grade, this disconnect was thought to be the result of his transition from a rural elementary school to a large middle school. Because he did so poorly that year, he is now placed in lower-level classes, and for the past six months has received weekly pull-out support for reading and writing within a tiered instructional system.

Enrique, Grade 3

Petra, Grade 5

Adonis, Grade 7

STUDENT PROFILES

JONELSI is a 14-year old girl at a large urban public high school. She has a daily evening babysitting job, and she plays trumpet in the school marching band. With the exception of her music class, she is failing all of her courses. She has been suspended twice for fighting in the cafeteria. In addition, she has served multiple detentions for inappropriate classroom behavior (talking rudely to teachers, making fun of other students, and playing practical jokes that interfere with classroom instruction). Jonelsi had done reasonably well academically in middle school, and though she occasionally got into trouble there, it was neither as serious nor frequent as it has been at high school. She does not complete homework, and does little work during the school day except when she works 1:1 with a teacher. She talks constantly to the students around her, and frequently interrupts the class with jokes or corrections (she is a "know-it-all" who enjoys pointing out and correcting the errors of teachers or other students). When asked to explain her difficulties, she says she is considering dropping out of school.

Jonelsi, Grade 9

NATHAN is a 17-year old boy at a competitive independent high school. He earns top grades in some courses and is failing others. He has a history of moderate academic struggles, and was on an IEP (individualized education plan) in his public middle school for math and writing (though he now earns top grades in Algebra II). He plays a varsity sport, sings in a choir, plays fiddle in a Celtic band, and is active both in his church and the school's community service program. He is well-liked and respected by adults and students. His parents and teachers are frustrated and confused by what they see as his lack of effort and motivation because he is clearly intelligent and able to do the work. He tells his guidance counselor that he's failing partly because he can't remember the minutiae that he is tested on, partly because he is bored by the reading and has a hard time completing it, partly because he doesn't like the teachers in those classes, and partly because he often gets distracted by his music and other activities and forgets what he is supposed to be doing until it is too late to complete it.

Nathan, Grade 11

In Their Own Words
Students with LBLD Talk about School

School was awful for me. I hated every minute of it. I didn't understand what was happening in class, it took me hours to complete homework, and I would fail tests, quizzes, and basically all of my academic classes. It was hard for me to tell everyone about my LD and I didn't want to because I thought I was the only one. When I came to my new school I realized that so many people have an LD. Now I am so comfortable and have no challenges in coming to school.

Elyse, high school student

I put off every assignment and leave it to the last minute because I always tell myself I have more time.

Garth, middle school student

One of the hardest things for me is listening and following class lectures and discussions if I am not interested or I really don't understand it. When I don't understand it I will stop listening to the conversation and I will think or do something else. I think it would help if the teacher would get the students involved or ask us questions to keep the focus.

Ratha, high school student

I've come to a frightening conclusion that I am the decisive element in the classroom. It's my personal approach that creates the climate. It's my daily mood that makes the weather. As a teacher, I possess a tremendous power to make a child's life miserable or joyous. I can be a tool of torture or an instrument of inspiration. I can humiliate or heal. In all situations, it is my response that decides whether a crisis will be escalated or de-escalated and a child humanized or dehumanized.
- Haim G. Ginott, teacher and psychologist

WHAT TO DO

No matter their grade level, the range of students' skills and knowledge is dramatic. In order to nurture their educational lives, we need to know them well: where they come from and what their lives are like, what they like and dislike about school, what they are good at and what they find difficult. We also need to learn about students' executive functioning because it profoundly influences how well they learn and demonstrate their learning.

Although many students enter our classrooms with individualized education plans (IEPs) or 504 plans in place to guide our instruction, most do not. Yet significant numbers of students (and teachers too) are challenged by weak executive functioning. Creating and using student questionnaires is an excellent way to help us gather useful information to guide our instruction.

Student Questionnaires

Questionnaires are easy to design and can provide a wealth of information. Many teachers use questionnaires at the beginning of each year or term to learn about students' interests and needs. Others use them throughout the year as a basis for student conferences and to help develop students develop self-awareness and self-assessment skills.

The simple questionnaires that follow invite immediate feedback from students on their perceptions of their executive skill. These self-reports can provide a rich source of informal diagnostic information, particularly when compared with the teacher's assessment based on classroom observation, and discussed in 1:1 conferences with students.

These questionnaires should not replace formal diagnostic assessment tools to be used with students suspected of having learning disabilities, attention disorders, or other difficulties. Modify or print these student questionnaires at www.landmarkoutreach.org/ef-resources. When you open this page, enter the username (**foundations**) and the password (**OUTREACH**).

Online Resource Available

STUDENT QUESTIONNAIRE

Executive Function Questionnaire
For Younger Students

Name: _____ **Date:** _____

Directions:

1. In the first box below, list at least three things you are good at doing.
2. Read, or have someone read to you, each category below, and the areas of difficulty that follow.
3. Mark an X for each statement that is true for you. If a statement is not true for you, leave it blank.

Strengths	List three things you are good at doing.

Getting Started	It is hard for me to get started on:
	My work at school
	My homework
	My chores at home
	A new task
	Reading, writing, or math work

Paying Attention	It is hard for me to:
	Pay attention when the teacher is talking
	Follow directions
	Pay attention to what I'm reading
	Do work when there is noise or others are talking
	Stop daydreaming

Trying	It is hard for me to:
	Keep working even when things get difficult or confusing
	Stay awake and pay attention
	Work fast
	Make sure I do all the steps needed to complete a difficult task
	Put effort into things I'm not interested in but must do

Continue to the next page →

Feeling	I often feel:
	Disorganized
	Frustrated
	Angry at myself or others
	Sad
	Overwhelmed with too many things to think about and do
Remembering	**I have trouble remembering:**
	Things I am supposed to do
	To bring things I need for school or other activities
	Information I have learned
	What steps to follow for tasks
	Words
Doing	**I have difficulty:**
	Checking my work to make sure it is correct and complete
	Finishing tasks
	Turning in my homework or class work
	Figuring out another way to do a task if my way doesn't work
	Keeping my things neat and organized
What Should I Do?	

Directions:

1. Circle the items you marked with an X that you wish you could improve or change.
2. In the space below, list any ideas you have about what you and your teacher could do to help you achieve your goals.

STUDENT QUESTIONNAIRE

STUDENT QUESTIONNAIRE: TEACHER VERSION

Executive Function Questionnaire For Younger Students
Teacher Form

Student Name: _____ **Date:** _____

Teacher Name: _____

- In the first section, identify three strengths (personal, academic, or extracurricular) you have observed in the student, and a specific example of how you observed the student demonstrate it.
- In the following sections, place a checkmark next to each area of difficulty you observe. Write NE if the category is one for which you have no evidence. Consider meeting with each student to compare their ratings with yours, and set goals for areas to address with strategies.

Strengths	Example of how student demonstrated strength

Getting Started	It is hard for student to get started on:
	Work at school
	Homework
	Chores at home
	New task
	Reading, writing, or math work

Paying Attention	It is hard for student to:
	Pay attention when the teacher is talking
	Follow directions
	Pay attention to what I'm reading
	Do work when there is noise or others are talking
	Stop daydreaming

Trying	It is hard for student to:
	Keep working even when things get difficult or confusing
	Stay awake and pay attention
	Work fast
	Make sure s/he does all the steps to complete a difficult task
	To do things s/he is not interested in but must do

Continue to the next page →

Feeling	Student often seems:
	Disorganized
	Frustrated
	Angry at him/herself or others
	Sad
	Overwhelmed with too many things to think about and do
Remembering	**Student has trouble remembering:**
	Things s/he is supposed to do
	To bring things s/he needs for school or other activities
	Information s/he has learned
	What steps to follow for tasks
	Words
Doing	**Student has difficulty:**
	Checking work to make sure it is correct and complete
	Finishing tasks
	Turning in homework or class work
	Figuring out another way to do a task if strategy doesn't work
	Keeping things neat and organized
	Plan

1. After you have collected the student's completed questionnaire, compare it with yours. Begin by noticing similarities and differences in areas of strength.

2. Identify items on which you and the student gave <u>inconsistent</u> ratings. Often, students underrate their abilities. Sometimes they overrate them. Discuss with the student the reasons for his/her answer, and make a plan to provide frequent and specific positive feedback on performance in the area(s) so the student can develop a better sense of his/her skills.

3. Identify items on which you and the student gave <u>consistent</u> ratings. Choose one or two areas of difficulty, and assist the student to set reasonable goals and make a step-by-step plan to achieve (and assess progress toward) those goals.

STUDENT QUESTIONNAIRE: TEACHER VERSION

STUDENT QUESTIONNAIRE

Executive Function Questionnaire
For Older Students

Name: _____ **Date:** _____

Directions:
- In the first section, list at least three strengths you have (academic, personal, and/or extracurricular). Include a specific example of each.
- Read, or have someone read to you, each category bar below, and the areas of difficulty that follow.
- Rate yourself on how true each statement is for you:

♦ **0=Never**   ♦ **2=Occasionally**   ♦ **3=Often**   ♦ **4=Usually**

Strengths	List at least three strengths you have, and a specific example of each:

Activation	It is hard for me to:
	Keep my stuff organized
	Prioritize my assignments and activities
	Get started on tasks that are difficult or take a while to complete
	Get started on tasks I'm not interested in
	Stop doing one thing when I need to get going on something else

Focus	It is hard for me to:
	Pay attention during lectures or discussions
	Follow complex directions or lots of steps to complete a task
	Pay attention to what I'm reading for school
	Do work when there is noise or others are talking
	Stop thinking about things that distract me from my work

Effort	It is hard for me to:
	Continue working even when things get difficult or confusing
	Stay awake and focused in class or when doing homework
	Work fast to complete a timed task or to slow down and be careful
	Make sure I complete all the steps required for a task
	Stay motivated to do things I'm not interested in but must do

Emotion	I often feel:
	Disorganized
	Frustrated with myself or others
	Angry at myself or others
	Sad
	Overwhelmed with too many things to think about and do

Memory	I have trouble remembering:
	Things I am supposed to do
	To bring things I need for school or other activities

	Information I have learned
	What steps to follow for tasks
	Words
Action	I have difficulty:
	Checking my work to make sure it is correct and complete
	Finishing tasks
	Turning in my homework or class work
	Figuring out another way to do something if my way doesn't work
	Keeping my things neat and organized

Reflect on Your Self-Assessment

The categories above reflect facets of executive function. While many people have occasional challenges with executive functioning, some also have more severe or persistent difficulties that interfere with success in school and at home, and can make them feel badly about themselves.

Directions:

Circle or highlight any item that you rated with a 3 or 4. In the space below, write about how these difficulties interfere with your ability to be successful. Add any ideas about what you and/or your teacher could do to help you get stronger in these areas.

STUDENT QUESTIONNAIRE: TEACHER VERSION

Executive Function Questionnaire for Older Students
Teacher Form

Student Name: _____ **Date:** _____

Teacher Name: _____

- In the first section, list at least three strengths you observe in the student (academic, personal, and/or extracurricular). Include a specific example of each.
- Based on your knowledge and observations of the student named above, rate him or her on each item below.
- Consider meeting with each student to compare their ratings with yours, and set goals for areas to address with strategies.

♦0=Never ♦2=Occasionally ♦3=Often ♦4=Usually ♦NBJ (no basis to judge)

Strengths	List at least three strengths you observe, and a specific example of each:
Activation	It is hard for me to:
	Keep my stuff organized
	Prioritize my assignments and activities
	Get started on tasks that are difficult or take a while to complete
	Get started on tasks I'm not interested in
	Stop doing one thing when I need to get going on something else
Focus	It is hard for me to:
	Pay attention during lectures or discussions
	Follow complex directions or lots of steps to complete a task
	Pay attention to what I'm reading for school
	Do work when there is noise or others are talking
	Stop thinking about things that distract me from my work
Effort	It is hard for me to:
	Continue working even when things get difficult or confusing
	Stay awake and focused in class or when doing homework
	Work fast to complete a timed task or to slow down and be careful
	Make sure I complete all the steps required for a task
	Stay motivated to do things I'm not interested in but must do
Emotion	I often feel:
	Disorganized
	Frustrated with myself or others
	Angry at myself or others
	Sad
	Overwhelmed with too many things to think about and do
Memory	I have trouble remembering:
	Things I am supposed to do
	To bring things I need for school or other activities

	Information I have learned
	What steps to follow for tasks
	Words
Action	I have difficulty:
	Checking my work to make sure it is correct and complete
	Finishing tasks
	Turning in my homework or class work
	Figuring out another way to do something if my way doesn't work
	Keeping my things neat and organized

Reflections on Assessments

Directions for Teachers:

Part 1: Circle or highlight any score of *3* or *4*. In the space below, write about how you observe these difficulties interfering with the student's success in the classroom. Add any ideas about what strategies you could teach the student to help him or her address these difficulties.

Part 2: After you have collected the student's completed questionnaire, compare it with your completed questionnaire. In the space below, identify the items on which you and the student gave <u>consistent</u> ratings of 3 or 4. Meet with the student to set goals for one or two of these areas, and a step-by-step plan to achieve (and assess progress toward) the goals.

Part 3: Identify any items on which you and the student gave <u>inconsistent</u> ratings. Often, students underrate their abilities, and occasionally they overrate them. In a supportive way, discuss these areas with students. Make a plan to provide specific feedback in each of these areas so that the student may increase self-awareness.

STUDENT QUESTIONNAIRE: TEACHER VERSION

12 EXAMPLE PRACTICES THAT ENHANCE EF

12 Example Practices That Enhance Executive Function

Must Include Explicit Instruction and Guided Practice to Establish Routines

Target Skill	Example Activity
Self-awareness building	Use learning reflection journals and questionnaires about strengths and needs, motivations, personality styles, thinking styles, and learning styles.
Goal-setting	Create goal-setting sheets for personal and academic goals.
Planning	Complete step-by-step planning sheets for meeting goals and write reflections on progress frequently.
Managing focus	Implement multisensory instruction, and plan to have students actively engaged with language (e.g., talking, writing).
Managing materials	Follow a materials management system for tools, and paper and digital academic files.
Managing time	Practice time estimation and self-assessment for common academic tasks. Use a strategic calendar system.
Managing language	Use a columned note-taking system (e.g., Cornell notes).
Managing memory	Use card-sorting activities and teach self-cuing techniques.
Managing emotion	Teach and practice mini-meditation sessions.
Managing effort	Stop work every 5-10 minutes and have students rate their effort levels.
Self-Assessing	Use self-assessment sheets, attach to work, and keep in learning journals.
Self-Advocating	Script, practice, and provide time for identifying and requesting needed assistance.

Chapter 2
Attention and Memory

WHAT TO KNOW

Attention

Researchers agree that executive function enables human beings to engage in goal-oriented behavior; however, there is currently no general consensus on how executive function actually functions. Because researchers use different words to describe brain processes and view the nature of executive function interferences and interventions differently, educators can become quickly confused in the effort to understand why their students are having difficulties in school and what to do about it. Researchers do agree, however, that attention is one key facet of strong executive function.

ADHD and Executive Function

The connection between attention deficit/hyperactivity disorder (ADHD) and executive function is one area of confusion among educators. Even the newest edition of the American Psychiatric Association's *Diagnostic Statistical Manual* (DSM-V)—the book qualified professionals use to guide their diagnoses—does not provide sufficient information about the relationship.

The symptoms described for ADHD reflect cognitive interferences associated with weak executive function (e.g., difficulties with sustained attention,

ADHD and executive function disorder are not the same thing. It is possible that in future editions of the DSM-V, the definition, diagnostic criteria, and explanation of ADHD will include specific information on the syndrome of executive function impairments.

sustained mental effort, follow-through, organization, inhibiting impulsive behaviors, etc.). Attention is only one facet of executive function. Unfortunately, the current diagnostic criteria for ADHD does not reflect the full spectrum of difficulties that weak executive function causes. Thomas E. Brown, M.D., of Yale University, points out that the DSM-V:

> ...does not very adequately reflect scientific advances in understanding ADHD that have emerged over the 13 years since the last revision...and does not adequately reflect the underlying cognitive difficulties, the syndrome of executive function impairments, which have been found to be the core of ADHD (July 5, 2013).

The questions most educators ask is, "Are ADHD and executive function disorder the same thing?" Many of us are more familiar with ADHD than executive function because ADHD was so prominent in the news during the 1990s when the media gave a great deal of airtime to debates about the best interventions to support children (i.e., whether medication was helpful or harmful, if diet played a role in symptomatology, etc.). Many researchers today understand that ADHD as it is currently described in the DSM-V reflects one facet of impairment in the executive system of the brain. The short answer to the question is no, ADHD and executive function disorder are not the same thing, but they are related.

It is possible that in future editions of the DSM-V, the definition, diagnostic criteria, and explanation of ADHD will include specific information on the syndrome of executive function impairments. Until then, both educators and parents should keep in mind the important section of the DSM-V that calls attention to the variability of ADHD that can make it (and executive function of course) difficult to understand and diagnose:

> Typically, symptoms [of ADHD] vary depending on context within a given setting. Signs of the disorder may be minimal or absent when the individual is receiving frequent rewards for appropriate behavior, is under close supervision, is in a novel setting, is engaged in especially interesting activities, has consistent external stimulation

(e.g., via electronic screens), or is interacting in one-on-one situations (e.g., the clinician's office) (American Psychiatric Association, 2013).

This description suggests what researchers know—ADHD is far more complex than the current diagnostic criteria recognizes.

Attention and Executive Function

Many medical professionals note the links between weak executive function and attention. Two of the most widely recognized in education are Russell A. Barkley and Thomas E. Brown. Both describe challenges associated with attention deficit/hyperactivity disorder (ADHD) in terms of executive function and recognize that both children and adults with attention disorders experience difficulties beyond focusing their attention—difficulties associated with executive function. Barkley and Brown are just two of many researchers striving to understand ADHD and executive function and guide people toward interventions that empower it.

Barkley locates the core of difficulty in response inhibition—that is, the control to stop or defer certain responses in order to identify a task and future goal, develop a plan, and maintain problem-solving behavior toward the future goal (2013, p. 7). Brown, on the other hand, takes the perspective that the various areas of executive function are equally important to goal achievement. Brown writes, "I believe that inhibition, the ability to put on the brakes, is just one aspect of executive function. Equally important are the brain's systems for ignition, transmission, and steering. All must interact to operate the car" (2005, p. 173). Both agree that the capacity for focused attention is one cognitive element managed by executive function.

What Is Attention?

Attention references the brain's skill at identifying relevant incoming sensory information in order to initiate and maintain focus for a defined period of time, and shift that focus as necessary.

> ADHD is far more complex than the current diagnostic criteria recognizes... children and adults with attention disorders experience difficulties beyond focusing their attention— difficulties associated with executive function.

> We cannot pay attention to everything simultaneously because individual consciousness has limited capacity... the ability to focus our attention is necessary to learning.

In a *Scientific American* article summarizing the importance of attention to learning, Engel, Debener, & Kranczioch (2006) looked back to William James's *The Principles of Psychology* (1890). James concluded that we cannot pay attention to everything simultaneously because individual consciousness has limited capacity. Though philosophers and psychologists like James have long been interested in attention, the increasing availability of neuroimaging technology has enabled neuroscientists a greater understanding of how attention works and the role it plays in learning. The ability to focus our attention and to know what to focus on is necessary to learning of any kind. This ability impels our consciousness to hone in on specific stimuli, which is necessary for effective processing (Engel, Debener, & Kranczioch, 2006).

What happens in our brains when we pay attention? Studies conducted in the 1980s connected attention to increased neuronal activity in the brain. Recent neurobiological research reports that the synchronization of neurons' increased activity is another significant factor. Nerve cells work as cooperative units, and only signals from teams of neurons that cooperate well are strong enough to reach consciousness. When we deliberately concentrate on something, neurons in the brain become highly active and their synchronization improves. The effect is "a symphony orchestra that soon arrives at a common tempo after the individual instruments begin playing" (Engel, Debener, & Kranczioch, 2006, p. 52). This analogy, like Brown's (2007), reflects investigators' interest in the extent of overlap between attention disorders and disorders of executive function.

When we focus our attention enough for information to penetrate our consciousness, memory comes into play. We use different types of memory for different purposes, and all are essential to learning.

Memory

Memory is the brain's skill at acquiring, storing, and accessing information. How memory works is the object of enthusiastic enquiry. An article from the Neuroscience Research Center at the University of Texas states: "The quest to understand the anatomical, biophysical, and molecular processes underlying learning and memory is one of the greatest challenges in neurobiology. The questions to be answered in this endeavor are as broad as they are complex" (Neuroscience Research Center [NRC], 2013). McGill University hosts an outstanding Web site that addresses the role memory plays in the learning process—*The Brain from Top to Bottom* (http://thebrain.mcgill.ca).

Memory and learning are different, but they depend on each other. Learning is a modification that happens when the brain absorbs new information and associates it with information stored in memory. Memory is the brain's ability to reconstruct what it has stored and reclassify it using new information. Figure 5 represents this description.

> Learning is a modification that happens when the brain absorbs new information and associates it with information stored in memory.

MEMORY AND THE LEARNING PROCESS

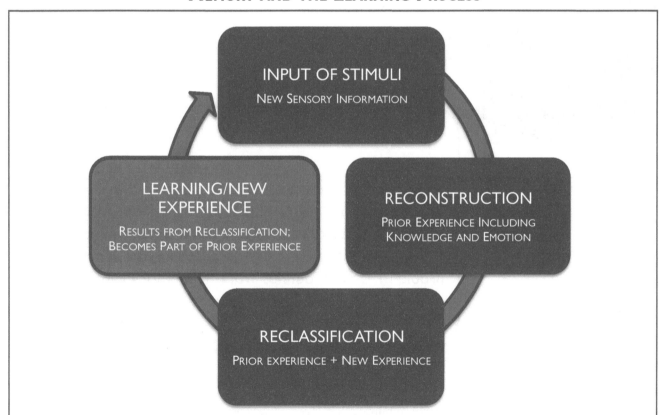

Figure 5. Memory and the learning process.

Scientists today view the act of remembering not as a simple retrieval of fixed records, but as an ongoing process of reclassification resulting from continuous changes in our neural pathways and parallel processing of information (NRC, 1994).

Types of Memory

There are different types of memory, and all are important to learning. There continues to be controversy among researchers and theorists about how the brain's memory systems should be described in relation to one another. While this book does not claim to promote one theory over another, it is helpful for educators to be familiar with three distinct and integrated aspects of memory: working memory; short- and intermediate-term memory; and long-term memory.

Working Memory

Working memory is closely linked to attention. Working memory allows us to manipulate different bits of information held in mind so we can do something with them. Doing mental arithmetic, memorizing a phone number, following a lecture, reading a magazine article, and writing an essay all require the focused attention and the use of working memory. Working memory has capacity and capability.

WORKING MEMORY CAPACITY AND CAPABILITY

Working memory capacity is the number of separate pieces of information an individual can hold in mind (e.g., the numbers and signs in an arithmetic problem). Working memory capability refers to how we organize and manipulate this information (e.g., solving the arithmetic problem). Cowan defines working memory capability as "how well attention can be used to keep a task goal active in the presence of interference" (2005, p. viii).

A common analogy for working memory capacity is a worktable. A project—constructing a mosaic, for example—requires space to lay out, organize, and use the materials so the artist can stay focused on realizing her vision. If the worktable is too small, materials may go missing, the artist may grow frustrated or anxious, and fulfilling the vision for the artwork becomes far more challenging.

No matter the size of the worktable—working memory capacity—the artist will have difficulty she cannot focus her attention on and organize the steps required to realize her vision—working memory capability. An individual's working memory capacity and capability can enhance or interfere with achieving any goal, including academic work. Weaknesses in working memory are often associated with disorders of language, attention, and executive function.

> Interferences with short- and intermediate-term memory profoundly impact learning and language production.

Short- and Intermediate-Term Memory

Short-term and intermediate-term memory provide storage of small bits of information for short periods of time—seconds to minutes. Their storage capacities are limited, but can be extended by chunking bits together. The terms are sometimes used interchangeably with working memory; however working memory refers to both ability to store and to process information. To extend the artist analogy above, the artist requires materials if she is to construct a mosaic on her work table. Information stored in short- and intermediate-term memory is analogous to the artist's materials. Without access to the necessary materials, the artist will be unable to realize her vision. Interferences with short- and intermediate-term memory profoundly impact learning and language production.

Long-Term Memory

Long-term memory allows us to hold information over extended periods—sometimes a lifetime. Contrary to the image many people have of long-term memory as a vast collection of archived data, most of our memories are actually reconstructions. They are not stored in our brains like books on library shelves. Actually, when we remember something, we reconstruct it from elements scattered throughout our brains. Scientists today view the act of

> Unlike declarative memory which requires conscious reconstruction, procedural memory seems unconscious. Actions guided by our procedural memory are automatic (including conditioned emotional responses).

remembering not as a simple retrieval of fixed records, but as an ongoing process of reclassification resulting from continuous changes in our neural pathways and parallel processing of information (NRC, 2013).

Reclassification

The reclassification process explains why we remember events differently as time passes and as we gain new knowledge and experiences. A seventh-grader will remember the oral presentation he gave yesterday vastly differently than he will remember it as a middle-aged man. Why? His many years of learning and life experience reclassify the event when he reconstructs it in retrospect. Reclassification not only allows learning to spiral forward; it also enables the development of executive function and self-efficacy because students learn strategies that lead to successful outcomes.

RECLASSIFICATION BEGINS ALMOST IMMEDIATELY

Reclassification doesn't require years, or even days. It can begin almost immediately. When a first-grader reads the word *beat* as *bate*, her teacher may offer a rhyme to help her remember how to decode it: "When two vowels go walking, the first one does the talking." If she is attending to the teacher's instruction and can understand the strategy the teacher has given her, she has learned something new. This is the process of reclassification. The next time the student encounters this word or another with double vowels, she may remember the teacher's correction (the process of reconstruction) and associate it with the rhyme in order to read the word.

Declarative and Procedural Memory

Long-term memory is made up of two systems: declarative memory and procedural memory (see figure 6). Declarative memory is our own unique body of knowledge. It consists of episodic memory and semantic memory. Episodic memory is knowledge (including emotions) gained through our personal life experiences. It might be imagined as "the stories we tell ourselves about ourselves." Semantic memory is our factual and conceptual knowledge base—the sum of what we know about the world from both direct personal experience and indirect experience (e.g., book learning).

Unlike declarative memory which requires conscious reconstruction, procedural memory seems unconscious. Actions guided by our procedural memory are automatic (including conditioned emotional responses). The automaticity results from the constant repetition of a motor or cognitive task. For example, most people tie their shoes or drink from a cup with seemingly no conscious thought. Their procedural memory for these tasks developed as a result of explicit instruction and practice provided by their caregivers over time.

Tasks that ultimately become automatic may initially be guided by declarative memory. Repetitive practice allows the brain to re-code the process into procedural memory. To illustrate the transition, contrast a preschooler and an adult tying their shoes. The preschooler may vocalize the strategies she's practicing (e.g., singing the bunny-ears song to guide her actions), while the adult

> Actions guided by our procedural memory are automatic (including conditioned emotional responses). The automaticity results from the constant repetition of a motor or cognitive task.

LONG-TERM MEMORY

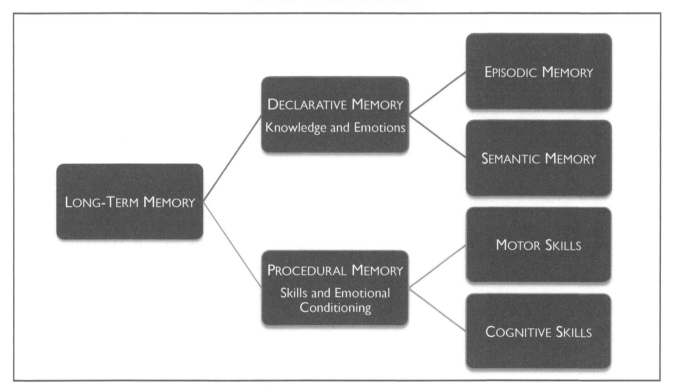

Figure 6. Long-term memory.

> Decoding text, is a cognitive task that starts out guided by explicit instruction and declarative memory. With enough practice, however, decoding skills are coded into procedural memory and become automatic.

may tie his shoes quickly, without looking, and while carrying on an unrelated conversation. This shift to automaticity indicates that the action has moved from the declarative memory to the procedural memory.

In addition to motor tasks, cognitive tasks can be coded into procedural memory. Decoding text, for example, is a cognitive task that starts out guided by explicit instruction and declarative memory. With enough practice, however, decoding skills are coded into procedural memory and become automatic.

MEMORY AND EXECUTIVE FUNCTION

The learning and practice of routines is an essential strategy to support memory and executive skill development. When we teach students to practice predictable routines for common tasks, these tasks become encoded in procedural memory. This frees up focused attention and working memory so that it can be devoted to higher level tasks such as comprehending what we decode.

Attention, Memory, and Executive Function

To learn, we must be able to:

• activate, focus, and sustain attention to take in new sensory information

• hold the new information in short-term memory and draw from long-term memory to reconstruct prior learning

• engage working memory to reclassify knowledge by associating the new information with what is already known

• store the reclassified knowledge (new learning) in long-term memory.

Our executive function allows us to initiate, regulate, and coordinate these cognitive tasks. Throughout this process, we must also regulate our emotional responses which can enhance or impede the achievement of a goal. Chapter 3 addresses the role of emotion in the learning process.

STUDENT PROFILES

The student profiles section of each chapter introduces different executive function facets of five students: Enrique, Petra, Adonis, Jonelsi, and Nathan. Each experiences difficulties in school that teachers must recognize, analyze and address. The profiles are composites of several actual students whose names have been changed.

Students have unique learning profiles that reflect their educational experience from the past and influence their current experience in school. Elements of their profiles include their learning, thinking, and personality styles; their emotion, motivation, and effort; and their particular areas of need for language acquisition and use. All students who struggle in school—particularly those with a learning disability—benefit from structured, multisensory, language-based skills instruction as well as opportunities to succeed. The student profiles in this book are included to encourage educators' thinking about and planning for the success of the students in their classes.

Consider Students' Attention and Memory

As you read about each student's attention and memory, keep in mind the following questions:

DOES THIS STUDENT HAVE DIFFICULTY WITH ATTENTION AND/OR MEMORY?

IN WHAT ENVIRONMENTS OR CONTEXTS DOES THE STUDENT HAVE DIFFICULTY?

WHAT INTERVENTIONS OR STRATEGIES WOULD I TRY TO HELP THE STUDENT BE MORE SUCCESSFUL?

Also think about your own students:

WHO AMONG MY STUDENTS SEEMS TO HAVE DIFFICULTY FOCUSING ATTENTION?

WHO AMONG MY STUDENTS DOESN'T RECALL LEARNED INFORMATION OR APPLY LEARNED STRATEGIES?

WHAT STEPS HAVE I TAKEN TO SUPPORT THESE STUDENTS?

WHAT SHOULD MY NEXT STEPS BE?

STUDENT PROFILES

STUDENT PROFILES

Enrique, Grade 3

ENRIQUE'S pediatrician evaluated him for ADHD by asking his mother and teachers to complete behavioral checklists. He did not qualify for a diagnosis, though concerns were raised about his level of anxiety. His teachers report that he needs frequent reminders to keep his materials organized and to transition more quickly between activities. He has difficulty sitting still during quiet reading and writing activities, and shows increasing intolerance for constructive criticism. Recently, he has begun to scribble on his returned work instead of making the corrections the teacher suggested. He has missed many days of school due to stomach aches and headaches. Though sometimes he is genuinely ill, other times his mother notices that he starts to feel better by mid-day and is anxious to go out to play with his friends. When his parents and teacher ask him about school, he says he is fine and he will try harder to do well.

Petra, Grade 5

At her father's request, PETRA, was evaluated for a learning disability. She reported how much she liked working with the evaluator. The academic evaluation indicated that Petra's cognitive potential falls into the superior range, and that her academic achievement on standardized assessments falls within grade-level expectations. The evaluator suggested that Petra might benefit from participating in the social skills group run by the school counselor, and in extracurricular activities. Petra is unable to participate after school because she is in charge of her younger brothers, but she attends the skills group during lunch periods once per week. The group leader reports that Petra will answer a direct question, but otherwise is very quiet and sometimes needs to be cued to listen to the conversation. Petra's teachers report that she never raises her hand to participate in discussion, and often says, "I don't know," when called upon directly. Petra's teacher has created a checklist of materials she needs to be prepared for school, and this has made a positive difference—she now remembers her lunch and books more regularly.

Adonis, Grade 7

ADONIS'S reading and writing skills have improved very little as a result of the support he receives. In a recent interim assessment, he scored lower than the previous year. He has been referred for an evaluation for a possible learning disability and, in the meantime, is receiving reading and writing instruction daily in a small group that meets with a reading specialist. He has begun complaining about going to school, and his grandmother notices a downward spiral in his attitude. He is argues more with her, and has been staying in his room more than usual.

JONELSI transitioned from a very small middle school in a suburb to a large urban high school when the family relocated because of her father's new job. Her parents are extremely worried about the changes in her behavior and her academic work. Jonelsi tells them she does not like school because the classes are dull, the teachers don't care and are mean, and everyone copies from each other. Occasionally, when her mother insists, Jonelsi sits with her to do work. At those times, she seems to understand and work efficiently. When she is in her room alone, she gets nothing done. The teachers with whom she has worked 1:1 report the same experience. She can do the work; however, she appears to have little motivation until she is forced. Jonelsi has been referred for a functional behavior assessment because her teachers are concerned that her classroom disruptiveness is becoming more severe. Although she gets laughs from other students in class and has developed a reputation as a tough kid—several students have commented, "You don't mess with her!"—she does not appear to have made any consistent friends.

Jonelsi, Grade 9

NATHAN was diagnosed with ADHD (inattentive type), executive function weaknesses, and math difficulties when he was in 6th grade at a public middle school. His IEP specified weekly counseling for anxiety, support in class from the inclusion specialist, extra time on tests, and the use of a calculator for math. A 3-month trial of medication was discontinued because he developed facial tics and interferences with appetite and sleep. In 7th grade, Nathan's difficulties intensified. His teachers noted that he would not take the initiative to ask for help, and he did not do homework consistently. His parents shared with teachers that Nathan commonly ripped up his homework, had angry and tearful outbursts when confronted with his online math homework, and several times left the house saying he was going to kill himself if he had to do any more math. His parents took him for additional counseling, and another trial of medication was discontinued after Nathan, his parents, and his teachers reported they noticed no differences in his ability to focus. By the end of 8th grade, Nathan had scored in the "Proficient" level of the state test, and had been accepted into an independent high school. Nathan's current teachers note that he is "great" in class; he actively participates in discussions, writes well, and takes good notes. They point out that his poor grades seem to be a result of inconsistent homework completion and the fact that he does not come for extra help even when asked to do so. Nathan has refused to take any medication, and becomes extremely angry when his parents try to facilitate his homework.

Nathan, Grade 11

STUDENT PROFILES

In Their Own Words
Students with LBLD Talk about School

People bugging me (distracting me) is the hard part. When people are talking, I can't concentrate. It's easier for me when no one is talking.

Adlin, elementary student

If I can do things in my own time, I remember. But when I'm being timed, like in math or on a test, everything just goes out of my head and all I can think about is why I can't remember what I know!

Sarah, elementary student

When the subject is interesting for me I will pay attention and listen, but if the subject is less interesting my mind just starts thinking about other things.

Adonis, middle school student

It was very difficult for me to participate in class or even friendly discussion when I was young because I was either not paying attention or did not understand what the other people in the situation were talking about.

Cathleen, high school student

The best way to learn is to do; the worst way to teach is to talk.

- Paul Halmos, mathematician

WHAT TO DO

Thousands of strategies exist for focusing attention and enhancing memory. Ironically, even teachers who implement a variety of strategies may be frustrated by some students' continued distractibility, impulsiveness, and forgetfulness. While it will not resolve all attention and memory interferences, well-planned and executed multisensory instruction enhances student focus, and helps map information and strategies into their long-term memory.

The key to multisensory instruction is finding ways for students to interact with the information and processes they are supposed to be learning. These interactions can be as exciting and intricately planned as a class simulation of a supreme court case, building a functional windmill, or staging a play. On the other hand, multisensory work needs to be neither complex nor time-consuming. Creating the game cards and playing *Password* to learn vocabulary, or highlighting, taking structured two-column notes and engaging in structured turn-and-talk activities are also examples of multisensory instruction.

Online Resource Available

Multisensory Instruction: Suggestions and Examples

Modify or print these sample activities at www.landmarkoutreach.org/ef-resources. When you open this page, enter the username (**foundations**) and the password (**OUTREACH**).

Five Suggestions for Multisensory Instruction

1. GET STUDENTS MOVING.

Example: Brainstorming prior knowledge and purpose(s) for learning

Instead of always handing students a K-W-L sheet, try a Round-Robin Brainstorm. Post large pieces of paper on the walls with the topic and subtopics. Place students in small groups to generate knowledge and questions on each sheet. At the end of a set time, have groups shift to the next paper, read what's written, and add more, to get exposure to and inspiration from others' ideas.

Example: Understanding Historical Concepts

Instead of only reading about a concept or looking at a diagram, try assigning students roles to research and act in for a simulation. To teach how a bill becomes a law, assign students roles to play, then simulate the process going from proposal to passage (or veto). To teach the impact of taxation without representation (the impetus for the American Revolution) assign roles to students and use pebbles or other small objects instead of money.

2. PRESENT ESSENTIAL CONCEPTS FROM THE SUBJECT IN MULTIPLE FORMATS.

Example: Understanding Shakespearean plays

Instead of only reading scenes, try watching different versions of them online and identifying the different interpretations, or try performing scenes.

Example: Understanding velocity and acceleration

Instead of reading about it and doing the calculations, try building ramps and vehicles, testing them out, and talking about how these activities make the math real.

3. MAKE SURE STUDENTS ARE DOING SOMETHING WITH INFORMATION AND IDEAS.

Example: Reading for homework

Instead of assigning only reading, try requiring students to list the main ideas on a sheet of notepaper, or place sticky-notes in the text with questions and ideas, or paraphrase the chapter summary.

Example: Reviewing for a quiz or test

Instead of reminding students to study, try putting key information or concepts on note cards or strips of paper, and ask students to categorize them (e.g., literary characters by quotes or traits, vocabulary with definitions, events with dates, or cause/effect).

4. INVITE OPTIONS FOR STUDENTS TO DEMONSTRATE THEIR KNOWLEDGE.

Example: Finding alternative ways to demonstrate learning

Instead of always giving a multiple choice or essay test, try discussing with students other ways they can demonstrate what they've learned. (e.g., writing a song or creating a mashup, writing/performing a play, creating a tabletop display, or creating a short film can fulfill the objectives you set.)

5. SOLICIT INPUT ON WHAT HELPS STUDENTS LEARN & PERFORM BEST.

Example: Questionnaires

Give students questionnaires that help both them and you gain a better understanding of their learning styles. (e.g., Are they more visual or auditory learners?)

Example: Assignment reflections

Ask students to reflect on different types of lessons you've implemented. What did they enjoy? What was difficult? What types of activities helped them understand and remember new information?

MULTISENSORY INSTRUCTION SUGGESTIONS

Paragraph Manipulatives

How can we get students to physically interact with language?

Try using paragraph manipulatives. This flexible strategy can be used across the curriculum, and provides a practical way to introduce or review information and ideas. Many teachers are surprised by the explicit thinking they observe when students in small groups discuss options for organizing manipulatives.

Other possible manipulatives activities include putting in order a cause and/or effect paragraph or a comparison and/or contrast paragraph. When practicing topic or concluding sentences with students, some teachers like to provide completed manipulatives with supporting details and have students write their own sentences on blank manipulatives. There are hundreds of possible uses for this type of language activity that calls on students to practice listening, speaking, reading, and writing skills.

STEP 1	**CHOOSE THE PARAGRAPH.**
	Write or find a paragraph that can be altered as a word document. Consider using paragraphs from the class's current texts if students need to review content.
STEP 2	**CREATE THE PARAGRAPH MANIPULATIVES.**
	Separate the paragraph into sentences so that, instead of flowing from one sentence to the next, each sentence is on its own line.
	Print out the document, and cut the sentences into strips with one sentence on each strip.
	Make one set for each group that will work together. Put the strips into envelopes to keep them together.
STEP 3	**DISTRIBUTE THE MANIPULATIVES.**
	Give the strips to students and have them work together to construct a paragraph in a manner that makes sense.

EXAMPLE

Full Paragraph:

There are many benefits to getting regular exercise. First of all, it can help you to build muscles and maintain a healthy weight. Similarly, exercising is good for your heart and overall health. Also, exercise can help to clear your mind of worries or stress. Finally, if you exercise with other people or play a team sport, you can develop valuable relationships and strengthen your emotional well-being. In conclusion, every person should find time each day to do something physically active.

continued on next page

PARAGRAPH MANIPULATIVES

SENTENCE MANIPULATIVES FROM PARAGRAPH

There are many benefits to getting regular exercise.

First of all, it can help you to build muscles and maintain a healthy weight.

Similarly, exercising is good for your heart and overall health.

Also, exercise can help to clear your mind of worries or stress.

Finally, if you exercise with other people or play a team sport, you can develop valuable relationships and strengthen your emotional well-being.

In conclusion, every person should find time each day to do something physically active.

Keryn Kwedor, Landmark High School, created this example of a paragraph manipulative activity. A version of it appears in Landmark Outreach's free e-resource, *Spotlight on Language-Based Teaching*.

PARAGRAPH MANIPULATIVES

Ideas for my classes:

Blank Sheet for Paragraph Manipulatives

PARAGRAPH MANIPULATIVES

Directions: Choose or write a well-constructed paragraph with a clear topic sentence, concluding sentence and supporting sentences with transition words. Write one sentence on each strip, photocopy enough for your class (or each small group), cut the strips, and put each set into an envelope. Distribute and tell students to organize the strips into a paragraph. This activity works well for writing instruction, as well as for reviewing key information from content areas.

Card Sorting Activities

How can we get students to physically interact with language?

Try using card sorting activities. Like paragraph manipulatives, card sorting is a flexible strategy that can be used across the curriculum for discovery instruction or skills practice. Card sorts can be done by individuals, or in small groups. Many teachers are surprised by the explicit thinking they observe when students discuss options for organizing the cards.

Other uses for sorting include categorizing cards into: main ideas and details of a social studies topic; steps of a scientific process; words and definitions for a world language; and characters and traits for a novel. There are hundreds of variations for this type of language activity that engage students in the practice of listening, speaking, reading, and writing skills. Though this sample activity includes no writing, teachers often have students create sorting activities for one another.

STEP 1	**PLAN. THINK ABOUT YOUR AUDIENCE.** How will they best interact with the activity? Is there anyone you are concerned about not working well with the activity? Anyone who might be lost, overwhelmed, bossy, etc.? Will you do the activity as a full class or small group? Will you pick the groups or let them? How much or how little instruction will you give them?
STEP 2	**INTRODUCE. LAY OUT THE EXPECTATIONS.** What is the goal? (You want to hear conversations in the groups. It is okay for them to politely disagree with each other. There may be many "right" ways to do the task.) What is the time frame to complete the task? What do students do when they are finished?
STEP 3	**LET GO. LET THE TASK HAPPEN** It may not be pretty at first—it is okay for them to be stumped for a little bit. Walk around and ask questions of the different groups. DO NOT inject how you would do it in any group—if a group is stumped, ask questions to get them to think about the task, visit another group and come back to make sure they are moving forward. If not, ask another question and repeat. Listen to the different conversations going on in each group, in order to have a sense of what will happen during the debrief.
STEP 4	**DEBRIEF. WHAT DID WE CONJECTURE, GENERALIZE, OR LEARN?** Make sure to leave time for this! Respond to what students are saying. Encourage comments from each group.
STEP 5	**FOLLOW-UP. WHAT DID YOU LEARN ABOUT HOW THE INDIVIDUALS THINK ABOUT THE CONCEPT?**

Jennifer Sauriol, Landmark High School, created this description of card sorting. Kathleen Hamon, Landmark High School, created the example that follows. A version of each appears in Landmark Outreach's free e-resource, *Spotlight on Language-Based Teaching*.

CARD SORTING

Sorting Numbers

This is a hands-on activity in which students categorize numbers (positive/negative) to reinforce their understanding of vocabulary. Teachers working with older students can utilize this same activity as students learn more of the real number system, including rational or irrational numbers, or even the complex number system.

STEP 1	**PREPARE CARDS** Prepare a set of cards with the numbers you would like students to interact with.
STEP 2	**DISTRIBUTE CARDS AND GIVE DIRECTIONS** Give each student or pair a set of cards. Have students sort them into piles (either based on their understanding or specific topics that you want them to focus on).
STEP 3	**REVIEW PILES/DEFINITIONS** Have students discuss what they found or give an example of one card that they put in each pile. Review the vocabulary related to each pile to add to students' understanding of the definitions.

EXAMPLE

If your goal is to have students discover, ask them to sort the cards into 2 or 3 piles and see what they focus on. From that, begin your lesson and help students create definitions. If you're reviewing a concept, ask students to sort into piles based on specific vocabulary.

EXAMPLE SORT:

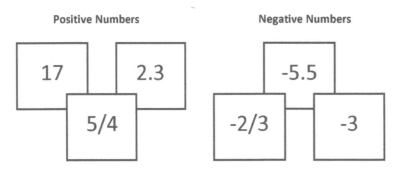

WANT TO USE THESE CARDS IN A DIFFERENT WAY?

- Have students put them in increasing or decreasing order.
- Have students play "war" with them, deciding which one is bigger.
- Have students place them on a number line.

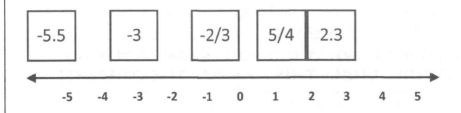

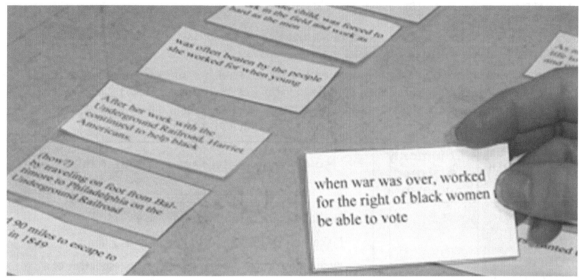

Sorting Events in Sequence

Sorting Pictures, Vocabulary, and Related Parts of Speech

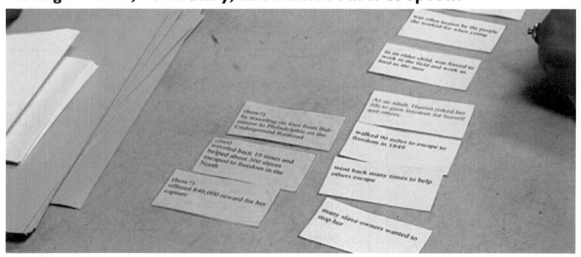

Sorting Questions and Answers

CARD SORTING EXAMPLES

MULTISENSORY HOMEWORK IDEAS

Multisensory Homework Assignments

Creating multisensory homework assignments facilitates students' success. Be clear about the purpose of the assignment first; then consider a variety of multisensory tasks to achieve it. Varying types of assignments offers students opportunities to excel in different ways. The grid below presents some examples to spur thinking about multisensory homework.

Homework Purpose	Commonly Assigned Homework	Multisensory Alternatives that Achieve the Same Purpose
Demonstrate understanding of a concept or event in history.	Write an essay.	• Create an interactive website. • Make a short (5-7 minute) documentary film. • Write a letter to the class from the perspective of a witness to, participant in, or key person related to the event. Include the major points that you want others to understand about it. • Create an online photo album with images and annotations that demonstrate your understanding of the concept or event.
Learn how to use particular mathematical formulas.	Practice plugging in information and solving for area, distance, or velocity.	• Measure the radius or length/width of common objects and calculate the area. • Measure the distance from one point to another and then time a car moving to calculate the average speed it traveled. • Measure two sides of a right triangle and then use the Pythagorean Theorem to find the third side. Check it by measuring the third side.
Learn or review characteristics of functions, numbers, operations, etc.	List characteristics of linear and quadratic functions.	• Complete a Venn diagram with similarities and differences between linear and quadratic functions, operations, types of numbers, etc. • Create a card game that reviews the characteristics of mathematical concepts.
Learn key ideas related to plot, setting, and character from a book	Read chapter.	• Read and make two-columned notes for characters/setting/plot. • Create a paper or poster with pictures or drawings and corresponding descriptions of setting/plot/characters and explain it to a partner. • Highlight characters, setting, and key events in three different colors while reading. • Use colored sticky-notes that correspond to characters, setting, or key events. Affix a setting note to the pages on which the author describes the setting, and write your question or comment on the note. Do the same for characters and key events.

Understand scene(s) from a Shakespeare play	Read scene(s) and translate to contemporary English.	• Watch several interpretations of the same scene on YouTube and write about how they are different. • Record yourself reading the scene out loud (alone or with friends). Then record yourself playing the scene with your own words.
Learn vocabulary words from a list	Study vocabulary.	• Make index cards (or use a free flashcard software such as Quizlet). Write the word on the front and a picture that reminds you of the definition. Write the definition and a sentence on the back. • Write a poem/story/song/mini-play that uses the vocabulary words. • Write the words on a piece of paper that you affix to a container (e.g., coffee can or oatmeal box). Fill the container with small objects or pictures that remind you of each word's definition. To review these words, dump out the objects and match them to the definitions.
Review for a test.	Study concepts from the chapter.	• Use an online discussion page/forum to interact with classmates and ask and answer questions. • Create note cards with major ideas or equations as a study guide.

Ideas For My Classes:

NOTES

Chapter 3
Emotion, Motivation and Effort

WHAT TO KNOW

Classroom experience tells us that students learn and perform best when they feel secure, confident, and engaged with class content. We also know that students' focus, learning, and performance suffer when they feel anxious, unsafe, or unhappy. This is not coincidental. Though cognition and emotion were understood as separate systems for centuries, advances in behavioral and neuroscience have contributed to a gradual change in this thinking. Scientific evidence shows that emotion is intricately interwoven with how we process incoming sensory information, how we react to the information (motivation), and how much effort we exert in reacting. Chapter 2 described the roles attention and memory play in learning. This chapter extends that description by exploring the influence that emotion, motivation, and effort have on the learning process.

While educators' focus is on teaching skills and content, the emotional context in which each student learns must inform both what and how we teach. When students react to instruction in ways that interfere with their success, we ought to ask ourselves, "Why?" The answer often lies in some facet of emotional processing.

Learning is influenced by past experience. Emotions are part of past experience; they color how we code incoming information and guide how we react to it. In class, when we teach, ask a question, or post an assignment, we set off a neurological chain of events that is unique to each of our students.

> In the simplest terms, cognitive processing—which includes emotion—means that our brains take in information, then respond to it.

Emotional Processing

In the simplest terms, cognitive processing—which includes emotion—means that our brains take in information, then respond to it. First, we perceive information through our five senses. Then, various parts of our brain code that information for further processing via unique networks of neurons that have been developing since we were born. In any learning situation, our executive function kicks in once our sensory system activates our neural networks and indicates that some action is required.

The sensory processing networks in our brain send messages to our memory networks. Our memory networks then reconstruct our past learning/experience and link up with our motivation networks. Our motivation networks, in turn, trigger a physiological response that dictates what level of effort we exert (if any) in our action. The experience is then reclassified in our memory so we can draw upon it for future action. Figure 7 summarizes this process. Although

STAGES OF EMOTIONAL PROCESSING

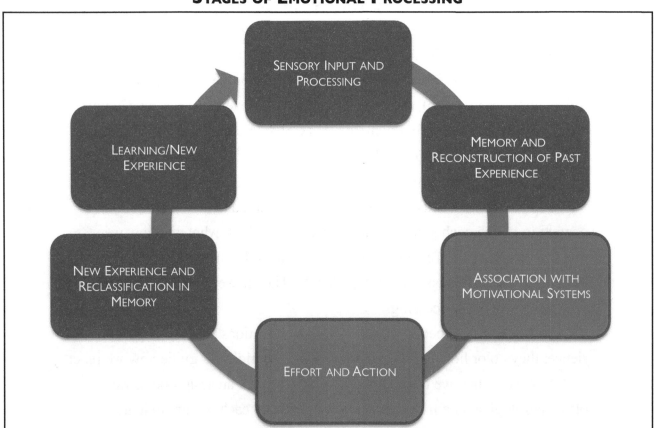

Figure 7. Stages of emotional processing.

similar to figure 5 in chapter 2, this figure adds emotion, motivation, and effort as part of the learning process.

Sensory Input

Our brains constantly register incoming sensory information and decide whether it requires us to act in some way. We do not focus on most of the input into our brains' sensory systems. Some, however, does alert us. If we had any past learning or experience with dogs, for example, the colors, shapes, and sounds of a snarling dog lunging at us would spur our memory networks to check on whether action was required, and what it should be. At the same time our brains also register and code the context of the sensory input. Is the dog part of a video game? Is it behind a tall, strong fence? Or is it really about to attack me? How we answer these questions influences our response.

Sensory Perception and Processing

Interferences with sensory perception or processing can cause interferences with other aspects of learning. Certainly, if one or more of our sensory perception systems are compromised, the input of sensory information is impacted. If no assistive devices are available, people with visual impairment must rely upon their other sensory systems for input, for example. The same is true for people with hearing impairment, or those with a sensory impairment of taste, smell, or feel.

> Interferences with sensory processing can cause interferences with other aspects of learning and action.

SENSORY PROCESSING AND EMOTION

Some individuals who experience interferences with sensory processing may experience physical discomfort, a sense of danger, and emotional distress that can lead to social and academic difficulties. These interferences can arise due to anxiety, depression, current or past trauma, and other issues.

> It is extremely important to recognize that some students have experienced or are currently experiencing trauma in their lives. If the trauma is unresolved, positive and effective emotional responses to sensory input may not occur.

Some people are able to perceive sensory input but may process it differently from others. Sensory processing disorder (also referred to as sensory integration disorder) is a term used to describe the difficulties of individuals whose sensory systems do not organize sensory input into appropriate motor and/or behavioral responses. As a result, these individuals may experience physical discomfort or even danger, emotional distress, and social and academic difficulties. While commonly seen on evaluations of students with school difficulties, sensory processing disorder is not a diagnostic category in the American Psychiatric Association's *Diagnostic Statistic Manual of Mental Disorders* (DSM-V). The APA's editorial group determined that more research is required to determine whether interferences with sensory processing constitute a distinct disorder, or are a feature of other disorders.

Additionally, excellent research on the effects of trauma on emotional processing continues to be done. It is extremely important to recognize that some students have experienced or are currently experiencing trauma in their lives. If the trauma is unresolved, positive and effective emotional responses to sensory input will not occur. Among a variety of effects that result from trauma, effective learning may be interrupted (D'Andrea, Ford, Stolbach, Spinazzola & van der Kolk, 2012). Bessel van Der Kolk, Founder and Medical Director of The Trauma Center at Justice Resource Institute in Brookline, Massachusetts and Peter A. Levine, Director of the Somatic Experiencing Trauma Institute in Boulder, Colorado have done excellent work in this area. See the recommended resources for further information on understanding and healing trauma.

Memory and Reconstruction of Past Experience

Almost simultaneously with sensory processing, our brains gather information from our memory networks to inform what (if any) action we should take. Chapter 2 highlighted the important fact that memory is dynamic rather than fixed. When we "remember," our brains actually reconstruct information from our various neural networks. Our short and intermediate-term memory hold this reconstruction and the new sensory input long enough for our working memory to compare them and decide upon action. This process often happens so quickly that we don't notice it.

When we are faced with the sensory input of a snarling, lunging dog, for example, our brains reconstruct information from declarative memory. We gather what we know about snarling, lunging dogs (attack is imminent) and what strategies we should use to react to them (turn to the side, move away slowly, don't stare). If we lack knowledge or strategies to draw upon, there is small likelihood of a successful outcome.

> A student who has learned—and can remember and use—the information and strategies he needs to complete a task successfully will gain confidence and increased skill.

Memory Reclassification

As chapter 2 explains, our memory constantly updates our past experience by reclassifying it to incorporate new experiences. This updating loop guides our reactions to any given situation. If our actions lead to a successful result, we will repeat them in the future, and perhaps become more confident about dealing with such challenges as a snarling, lunging dog. If the dog attacked us, however, our future encounters with dogs are likely to elicit fear and avoidance.

For many students, school work is similar to a snarling dog. A student who has learned—and can remember and use—the information and strategies he needs to complete a task successfully will gain confidence and increased skill. A student who is assigned a task but lacks (or cannot remember) knowledge about it or strategies to implement it will likely experience an unsuccessful outcome. Perhaps other students laugh at her attempt, or she earns a failing grade, or an adult makes a negative comment about her efforts. Whatever the result, the memory of a negative experience will influence her reaction to similar tasks in the future.

> Negative emotions from past experiences may induce a stress reaction that interferes with our ability to respond to a situation or task in an effective way.

Memory Interferences

There are scores of causes for memory interferences. People with attention disorders, for example, are commonly impeded by difficulty focusing their attention, reconstructing previously learned information, and using working memory. Even if they have learned material, they may not be able to remember or use it.

LBLD and Memory

People with unremediated language-based learning disabilities often lack automaticity when performing cognitive tasks such as decoding or encoding language. Unlike fluent readers or spellers who can rely on a quick and automatic response from procedural memory, they must consciously reconstruct from declarative memory what they need to read and spell with accuracy. As the language demands of school increase in volume and complexity, their memory systems can become overtaxed. They may become too exhausted to engage in the simultaneous comprehension and higher level thinking skills required as they move through school.

Stress and Memory

Stress also interferes with memory. Stress of any sort disrupts the focus needed during the initial phases of attention and memory reconstruction when our brains are processing sensory information. For example, a student who experiences stress because he is thirsty, or tired, or afraid, may be unable to process incoming information effectively. In addition, students trying to learn in a noisy classroom may be less successful than they would in a quieter context.

Emotion and Memory

Negative emotions from past experiences may induce a stress reaction that interferes with our ability to respond to a situation or task in an effective way. A student who has failed at a task, or been teased about her performance in the past may experience a stress reaction when asked to do something similar. Even if she currently has the knowledge and strategies to be successful, she may refuse or find other ways to avoid the task. As a result, when the experience is reclassified in memory, she has only reaffirmed her negative prior experience and may avoid similar tasks in the future.

Association with Motivational Systems

Once we code the sensory information and reconstruct past experience, our brains associate this information with information from our motivational systems. The most basic of our motivational systems are the appetitive and the defensive. Because we are bio-logically wired to survive, we seek what contributes to our survival (appetitive) and avoid what threatens it (defensive). Our reactions in any given situation (some by instinct, some by conscious choice) correlate with our perception of whether the consequence of our behavior will be pleasant/positive or unpleasant/negative. In the case of the snarling dog, our defensive system is motivated. We want to avoid the unpleasant consequence of being attacked.

Motivation dictates how much effort we put into action, what makes us choose one course of action over another, and what influences how long we persevere in the action.

Motivation

In an overview of motivational theories, Richard W. Scholl, a professor of organizational behavior at the University of Rhode Island (2002) proposes that motivation is what energizes, directs, and sustains our behavior. It dictates how much effort we put into action, what makes us choose one course of action over another, and what influences how long we persevere in the action.

Theorists pose many concepts about what motivates people, and it is beyond the scope of this section to summarize all of them. All generally point out that we can be motivated to particular action by internal and/or external forces, and by behavioral, cognitive and/or affective processes.

Internal and External Motivation

Internal motivation refers to the desire to do something because it gives us pleasure or helps us develop into the kind of person we want to be. For instance, a student may read a book about civil rights because he enjoys the stories, because he thinks that reading

> Behavioral motivation is a conditioned response to the input of information. Cognitive motivation refers to desires that result from conscious thinking processes. Affective motivation refers to desires that result from emotions.

it will advance him toward the well-educated person he wishes to be, and/or because he thinks it is important to learn about civil rights because he values the concept of freedom for all. Or, he may avoid reading because it is not pleasurable or he sees no purpose in it.

External motivation refers to the desire to engage in behavior because it leads to an external reward that we desire. For instance, the student may read the book about civil rights because he wants praise from his teacher for taking the initiative to extend his learning, or because he wants to earn an A on his history quiz, or because he is competing for a prize for an essay on civil rights and the book provides important information he needs.

Behavioral, Cognitive and Affective Motivation

Behavioral motivation is a conditioned response to the input of information. Some behaviors are involuntary responses to stimuli; for example, we squint in bright light. These types of involuntary responses can be conditioned by manipulating the environment. Other behaviors are voluntary responses to stimuli to which we have been conditioned. Many of our actions are motivated by behavioral conditioning—we drink coffee in the morning because it makes us feel more alert, we reach for medicine to make our headaches go away, or we avoid eating onions because they cause stomach upset. We are conditioned to seek pleasure/reward and avoid displeasure/negative consequences, so we learn to act accordingly. Sometimes a system of rewards and/or negative consequences can be created to condition desired behaviors. Often referred to as behavioral modification, it is a common approach used in the classroom.

Cognitive motivation refers to desires that result from conscious thinking processes. For instance, when a student is working on a long-term project for history class and she suddenly remembers she has a math test the next morning, she might weigh the pros and cons of continuing with her project versus stopping and reviewing for her test in order to identify what action she desires to pursue.

Affective motivation refers to desires that result from emotions. For instance, a student who is enjoying reading a novel for English class may desire to continue reading instead of studying for her science test. If she has robust executive function, her cognitive motivation will engage to help her determine what action will help her achieve her goal.

MOTIVATIONAL COMPLEXITY

Most of our desires result from a complex combination of internal, external, behavioral, cognitive and affective motivations. Individuals' motivation to act in any given situation can vary dramatically because desires are unique to learning and thinking styles, personalities, and life experiences.

Maslow's Hierarchy of Needs

What else guides our motivations? Abraham Maslow remains the most popular of the many theorists who have proposed models of motivation. His hierarchy of needs (1948; 1971 and Koltko-Rivera, 2006) describes motivation as arising from deficiency needs and growth needs. We are motivated to act in order to meet these needs, and the hierarchy of our deficiency needs must be met before we are motivated to meet our growth needs. Our physiological survival needs must be filled before we will be motivated to meet any other needs. Figure 8 summarizes Maslow's hierarchy.

Educators may find Maslow's hierarchy informative to understanding student motivation. In school, we aim for students to be motivated by the need to know and understand, but if their basic needs are not being met, they will be more motivated to meet those needs than to engage in learning behavior. Maslow writes that if someone is hungry:

> *all other needs may become simply non-existent or be pushed into the background...All capacities are put into the service of hunger-satisfaction, and the organization of these capacities is almost entirely determined by the one purpose of satisfying hunger...Capacities that are not useful for this purpose lie dormant, or are pushed into the*

We aim for students to be motivated by the need to know and understand, but if their basic needs are not being met, they will be more motivated to meet those needs than to engage in learning behavior.

> Classroom interactions frequently motivate students to behave in ways that mystify teachers. Students who appear unmotivated are simply not motivated to do what the teacher wants them to do.

background. The urge to write poetry, the desire to acquire an automobile, the interest in American history, the desire for a new pair of shoes are, in the extreme case, forgotten or become of secondary importance (1943).

Motivation in the Classroom

While most people would be motivated to act similarly if faced with a snarling dog that is lunging toward them, classroom interactions frequently motivate students to behave in ways that mystify teachers. In *The Motivation Breakthrough* (2007), Rick Lavoie reminds us that everyone is motivated. They may not be motivated to do what we want them to do, but they are motivated.

Why doesn't Gabriel do any reading or writing or seem to care that he is failing? Perhaps he feels better being seen as the tough problem kid than taking the risk people will find out he has trouble reading and writing. His need for the esteem of his teacher and peers takes precedent over his need to learn. Why does Sallie pinch and kick her classmates when lining up for lunch? Perhaps she wants to avoid going to the cafeteria. For her, the unpleasantness of eating in the principal's office is actually less unpleasant than the feelings of insecurity or loneliness she feels amid the noise and confusion of the middle school lunchroom.

Children and adolescents are often motivated by what Maslow describes as deficiency needs (physiological, safety, belongingness and love, and esteem). These must be met before their growth needs will motivate them. As teachers, we strive to motivate students to learn. Creating a classroom culture which meets their basic needs benefits all of us. We can do this by ensuring their physical comfort, creating a safe space in which they can confidently ask questions and make mistakes free from ridicule or belittlement, and implementing instruction that builds on students' strengths, involves them in the learning process, and values each individual student.

MASLOW'S HIERARCHY OF NEEDS

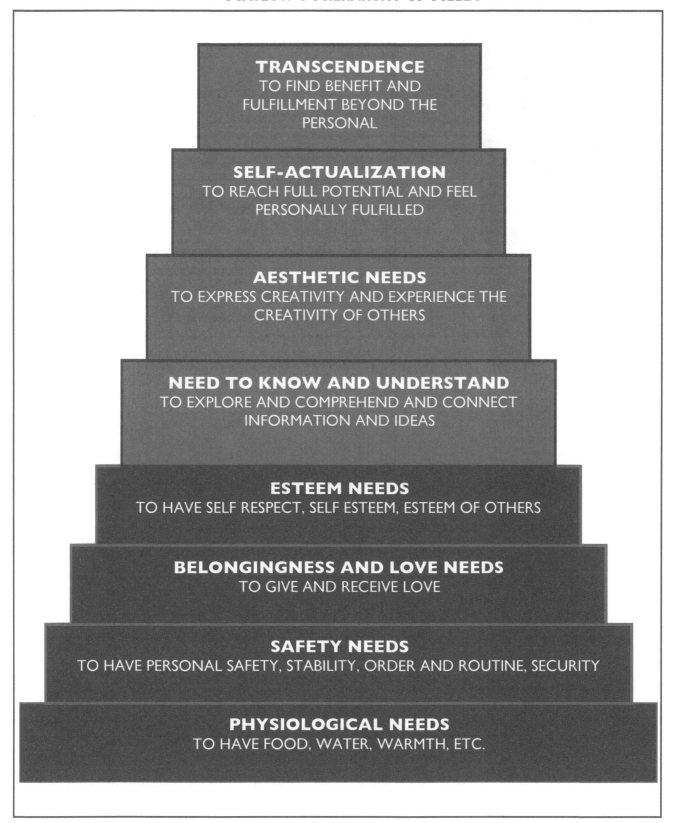

TRANSCENDENCE
TO FIND BENEFIT AND FULFILLMENT BEYOND THE PERSONAL

SELF-ACTUALIZATION
TO REACH FULL POTENTIAL AND FEEL PERSONALLY FULFILLED

AESTHETIC NEEDS
TO EXPRESS CREATIVITY AND EXPERIENCE THE CREATIVITY OF OTHERS

NEED TO KNOW AND UNDERSTAND
TO EXPLORE AND COMPREHEND AND CONNECT INFORMATION AND IDEAS

ESTEEM NEEDS
TO HAVE SELF RESPECT, SELF ESTEEM, ESTEEM OF OTHERS

BELONGINGNESS AND LOVE NEEDS
TO GIVE AND RECEIVE LOVE

SAFETY NEEDS
TO HAVE PERSONAL SAFETY, STABILITY, ORDER AND ROUTINE, SECURITY

PHYSIOLOGICAL NEEDS
TO HAVE FOOD, WATER, WARMTH, ETC.

Figure 8. Maslow's hierarchy of needs. Deficiency needs are shown in blue boxes; growth needs are shown in red boxes (Adapted from Huitt, W. 2011).

> Effort refers to the energy we expend to carry out an action. Effort is expended in intensity and duration.

STUDENT MOTIVATION

With few exceptions students are motivated to succeed in school. Students who do not experience reasonably consistent success as a result of their efforts over time develop changes in motivation and behavior. Adults exacerbate this dynamic when they misunderstand the cause and accuse students of lack of motivation and effort. Rather than investigating and addressing external causes for lack of motivation and effort (e.g., basic needs unmet, inadequate instruction, traumatic experiences, depression, etc.), many adults blame the student. When this happens, the student experiences an even deeper sense of inadequacy that reinforces the very behavior that prevented success in the first place.

Effort and Action

Effort and action, two facets of executive function, are closely linked to motivation. A hallmark of emotional processing is physiological activity (Bradley, 2000, p. 614). After our sensory, memory, and motivational systems are involved, our brains arouse us to exert effort. Effort refers to the energy we expend to carry out an action. Effort is expended in intensity and duration.

Emotional Arousal and Valence

Emotional response intensity is described in terms of arousal and valence. Arousal ranges from neutral to extreme, and relates to our physiological response to sensory input. Valence refers to our perception of how much pleasure or displeasure it will cause (Lewis, P.A. et. al. 2007). Some of our responses are instinctive (e.g., when we move our hand away from scalding water), while others are conscious (e.g., when we make a final sprint in an attempt to cross the finish line first).

When faced with a snarling dog, we would become highly

aroused and respond with increased heart rate and blood flow, and a release of adrenaline to fuel our effort to act. We would be further prepared to exert intense effort because we know the potential for profound displeasure should the dog attack.

Activation and Perseverance

Activation and perseverance of effort are both facets of executive function because they are necessary to goal achievement. We must initiate goal-oriented behavior *and* persevere in our efforts until we achieve the goal. Anyone who has tried to lose weight or commit to an exercise routine will quickly grasp the difference between activation and perseverance. While some people have difficulty getting started but little trouble once they do, others begin with enthusiastic effort only to give up before they've reached their goal. Researchers tend to agree that initiation of behavior is more related to affective motivation (emotion) while persistence of effort may be more related to cognitive motivation (goal-orientation) (Huitt, W., 2011).

> Initiation of behavior is more related to affective motivation (emotion) while persistence of effort may be more related to cognitive motivation (goal-orientation) (Huitt, W., 2011).

Memory and New Experience

Our actions in response to input of sensory information affect our memory. We reclassify what we used to know and store it in long-term memory. For example, if the snarling dog calmed down or backed off as a result of our action, the next time we encounter a similar situation, we will employ these same strategies more quickly and confidently. If the dog attacked, our memory is reclassified in a different way. Our strategy knowledge and use was not effective enough, and we had a traumatic experience that reclassifies our memory of dogs. In the future, we may avoid dogs altogether, or freeze with panic if a dog comes near us. Either of these actions reinforces our negative feelings about dogs, decreases our sense of self-efficacy, and prevents us from learning to respond effectively to a snarling dog.

> Students with underaddressed learning disabilities or a history of academic struggle are likely to have different responses to classroom expectations than students who have a history of success in school. What may appear to others as laziness, lack of motivation, insufficient effort, or active resistance is usually some form of fear of failure.

Student Experience Informs Future Learning and Performance

Students' experiences (memories) inform their cognitive, emotional, motivational and effortful responses in the classroom. Students with underaddressed learning disabilities or a history of academic struggle are likely to have different responses to classroom expectations than students who have a history of success in school. What may appear to others as laziness, lack of motivation, insufficient effort, or active resistance is usually some form of fear of failure.

The Failure Cycle

If a student does not succeed at an attempted task, the experience is negative, and they enter the failure cycle for that task (see figure 8). If the failure cycle is not interrupted shortly after a failed effort, the student's attitudes and behaviors begin to change. These changes quickly interfere with successful learning. Though many teachers attribute failed attempts to lack of motivation and effort, figure 8 demonstrates that loss of motivation actually comes very late in the cycle. To interrupt the failure cycle, a teacher must appropriately intervene at the frustration point so that the student can make another attempt at the task before further negative emotions complicate the process.

Once a student becomes enmeshed in the failure cycle and misses opportunities to become skilled enough to succeed at a task, they lose self-esteem and become victims of what is commonly called the Matthew Effect. Coined by Robert C. Merton (1968), the term refers to the phenomenon of accumulated advantage for some and accumulated deficit for others (e.g., the rich get richer and the poor get poorer).

In terms of academics, this means that the gaps between successful students and those who get stuck in the failure cycle become ever wider unless appropriate interventions are implemented. Students who are successful at reading, for example, are motivated to read more often and feel confident enough to attempt ever more challenging texts. Their skills increase with practice, and their body of knowledge grows. Students who struggle with

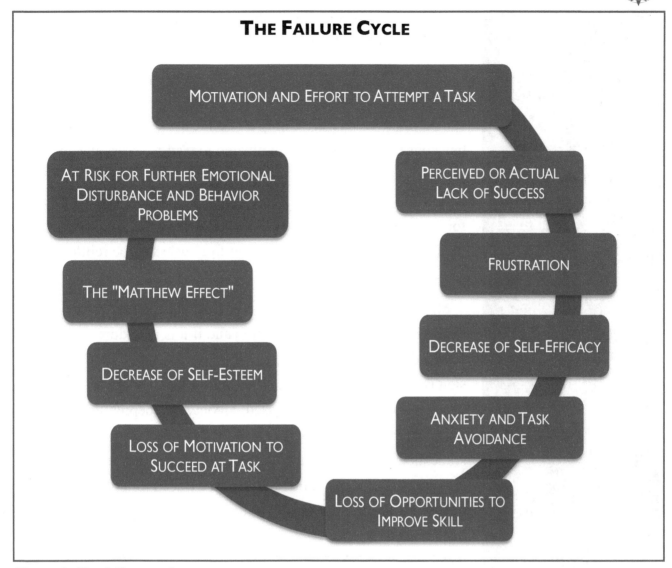

Figure 9. The failure cycle.

reading and are not receiving effective intervention, on the other hand, may become motivated to avoid it and miss opportunities to improve their skills. The gaps between them and their successful-reader peers grow ever wider.

Changes in behavior and attitude may relate only to a particular task such as reading, or generalize to related tasks such as writing, doing homework, or taking tests. If caught in the failure cycle on too many tasks, some students may even disengage from activities and interactions unrelated to academics, or turn to other self-destructive behaviors. This downward spiral of behavior and attitude links directly to the student's actual or perceived lack of success. Entrapment in the failure cycle is one of the reasons that

Students caught in the failure cycle may exhibit learned helplessness, a behavior in which they are motivated to wait for assistance on a task because they have learned they cannot be successful independently. Students caught in this cycle may not attempt a task or ask for help until they are forced to do so.

students with learning disabilities exhibit significantly higher rates of social, emotional, and behavioral problems.

Learned Helplessness

As a result of decreases in their sense of self-efficacy, students caught in the failure cycle may exhibit learned helplessness, a behavior in which they are motivated to wait for assistance on a task because they have learned they cannot be successful independently. Students caught in this cycle may not attempt a task or ask for help until they are forced to do so. If the proper scaffolding for their success is not in place, the passive cycle will be reinforced.

Anxiety and Depression

Many students who get caught in the failure cycle also develop anxiety and depression. Over time and if it is not addressed and resolved, anxiety can lead to depression. One hallmark of depression is a decrease in the ability to activate or sustain goal-oriented behavior. When left unaddressed, anxiety and depression have dangerous consequences; it is essential to investigate whether students who appear "unmotivated" are suffering from it, or if their apparent lack of motivation can be traced to unmet basic needs, or enmeshment in the failure cycle or the cycle of learned helplessness.

ANXIETY

Anxiety can manifest in a variety of ways including: task avoidance, irritability, emotional outbursts, diminished or excessive activity, somatization (i.e., feelings of pain or illness that seem to have no physical cause), and dissociation (e.g., "spacing out," day dreaming, etc.). Even minor levels of anxiety can profoundly disrupt the learning process.

Emotional Intelligence

In 1995, Daniel Goleman published *Emotional Intelligence*, a highly successful attempt to synthesize multiple strands of scientific research. Researchers from various disciplines continue to study and refine theories about intelligence, why cognitive ability does not always correlate with learning or performance, and the interrelationship between cognition and emotion. In a 2007 editorial, Oshsner and Phelps noted, "data have demonstrated that emotion and cognition not only interact, but that their integrative operation is necessary for adaptive functioning" (p. 317).

Perhaps most important to educators is research on the effectiveness of teaching social skills and emotional awareness, and the impact of this teaching on academic performance. A recent meta-analysis investigated the impact of social and emotional learning (SEL) programs at the K-12 levels. Hundreds of schools and thousands of learners were involved, and participants demonstrated significantly improved social skills, emotional "intelligence," attitudes, behavior, and academic performance (Durlak, Weissberg, Dymnicki, Taylor, & Schellinger, 2011).

The proliferation of programs and resources dedicated to learning how to live mindfully reflects growing awareness of the role emotion plays in learning and overall health. Jon Kabat-Zinn, founder of the Mindfulness-Based Stress Reduction program at the University of Massachusetts Medical Center, defines mindfulness as "paying attention in a particular way; on purpose, in the present moment, and nonjudgmentally" (2012, p. 1). Mindfulness meditation does not require adherence to any specific spiritual tradition, although it is rooted in Buddhism. Yoga and mindfulness meditation are gaining traction in schools as regular classroom practices. In a recently-released documentary film, *Room to Breathe*, filmmaker Russell Long documents the benefits of providing students with opportunities and instruction for mindful meditation.

> Yoga and mindfulness meditation are gaining traction in schools as regular classroom practices.

SUCCESSFUL LEARNING

A key foundation for successful learning is a safe, success-oriented teaching environment in which students consistently experience support and respect from the teacher and other students, are taught to give those in return, and learn explicitly about the roles emotion, motivation, and effort play in their learning experience.

STUDENT PROFILES

STUDENT PROFILES

The student profiles section of each chapter introduces different executive function facets of five students: Enrique, Petra, Adonis, Jonelsi, and Nathan. Each experiences difficulties in school that teachers must recognize, analyze and address. The profiles are composites of several actual students whose names have been changed.

Students have unique learning profiles that reflect their educational experience from the past and influence their current experience in school. Elements of their profiles include their learning, thinking, and personality styles; their emotion, motivation, and effort; and their particular areas of need for language acquisition and use. All students who struggle in school—particularly those with a learning disability— benefit from structured, multisensory, language-based skills instruction as well as opportunities to succeed. The student profiles in this book are included to encourage educators' thinking about and planning for the success of the students in their classes.

Interventions to Foster Positive Learning Experiences

As you read about each student, keep in mind the following questions about emotional processing:

> WHAT SORTS OF DIFFICULTIES DOES THIS STUDENT HAVE WITH EMOTION, MOTIVATION, AND EFFORT?

> IN WHAT CONTEXTS OR ENVIRONMENTS DO DIFFICULTIES EMERGE?

> WHAT INTERVENTIONS OR STRATEGIES WOULD I TRY TO HELP THIS STUDENT BE MORE SUCCESSFUL?

Also think about your own students:

> WHO AMONG MY STUDENTS SEEMS TO BE STRUGGLING WITH EMOTION, MOTIVATION AND EFFORT?

> WHAT STEPS HAVE I TAKEN TO SUPPORT THESE STUDENTS?

> WHAT SHOULD MY NEXT STEPS BE?

Enrique, Grade 3

ENRIQUE frequently visits the school nurse asking to go home because his stomach hurts or he gets headaches. The pediatrician has examined him and found nothing wrong. His eyes have been tested and he does not require glasses. His mother reports that he sleeps well, but probably does not eat enough healthy food. When she talks with him about how school is going, he says it would be better if he could be in the same readers' circle with his friends and if the other kids would stop making fun of him for being dumb. He says it makes him want to punch them, but he doesn't want to get in trouble. He also says he is embarrassed when the teacher gives back papers with corrections and everyone can see how many errors he made. It makes him feel like giving up when he sees other kids with high grades and only a few corrections, but his corrections always take a long time to make.

Petra, Grade 5

One day in the social skills group, PETRA began shouting at the other participants, then ran away from the group. They had been grumbling about their after school activities and complaining about what their mothers give them for after school snacks. Petra, shaking and angry, yelled that they should shut up and know that some people wish they could participate in extracurriculars, and some people wish they had a mother who would give them a snack even if it was a wrinkled old apple or gross cookies. The counselor asked another teacher to watch the group, and found Petra sobbing over the water fountain. She led her to an office to talk. She learned that two years earlier, Petra's mother had died of a drug overdose. Petra's father works two jobs, so Petra is in charge of taking care of the house and her younger brothers, 8 and 6. Afterwards, Petra became very upset that she had revealed this, and begged the counselor not to tell her father. It became clear to the school counselor that immediate intervention was required to support Petra and her family, and she talked with Petra about it.

Adonis, Grade 7

ADONIS'S grandmother was relieved when Adonis was diagnosed with a reading disorder and a disorder of written language. She knew he was smart but could never understand why he did so poorly in school. She assures Adonis that his teachers now know exactly what to do to help him improve his skills. Adonis is not happy with the diagnosis or the decision to move him to a specialized language-based classroom. He wants to be in class with his friends. He is angry and feels tired of explaining to them why he can't be. He tells his friends if he behaves badly enough, they won't want him in that class. Soon, he is in disciplinary meetings for throwing things at other students.

STUDENT PROFILES

STUDENT PROFILES

Jonelsi, Grade 9

JONELSI has been suspended twice for behavior, and has been told she will no longer be able to play in the marching band if she continues to miss rehearsals for any reason. She has also lost her babysitting job. She will likely need to go to summer school. Jonelsi's parents have spoken with her advisor as well as the school guidance counselor. Both said that they had asked Jonelsi to meet with them but she did not come at the appointed time. After contacting Jonelsi's 8th grade teacher (a family friend) to ask for advice, her parents decided to schedule Jonelsi for a neuropsychological evaluation. To their surprise, the evaluator indicated that Jonelsi meets the diagnostic criteria for ADHD of the mixed type, shows weaknesses in language processing, and scores in the high risk range for anxiety. The evaluator noted that Jonelsi expressed frustration at the difficulty of learning in such a noisy environment with large classes. In middle school, she had only 18 students in her class, and her teachers spent a lot of time with each student. She is having trouble understanding the extensive reading she is required to do, and struggling with "vague" writing assignments she is given. Jonelsi also reported feeling frightened about being in school after several incidents at the beginning of the school year, and her desire to prove to others that she is just as tough as they are.

Nathan, Grade 11

NATHAN tells his parents and counselors that he dislikes school and the only reason he attends is he enjoys the extracurricular activities and some of his teachers. He is very angry about failing math for the quarter because he is not allowed to use a calculator (his independent school does not honor his IEP from middle school). When his parents and counselor asked whether he had approached the teacher to discuss calculator use, he said he tried once early in the year and was told no. He says he would prefer to never speak to the teacher again. He is also upset about failing history because of a missing major paper. He thought he turned in all his work. He does not want to go to the teacher because, "She will just say it was my responsibility and I should have done it, and it will just make me mad, and it's too late anyway." He writes his assignments in an agenda and is quite successful keeping up in Spanish and physics. He always does those assignments first. He says he procrastinates on reading and writing assignments which seem like they will take hours and will prevent him from working on his screenplays, short stories, and a new film project. Because he does not complete these, he is also failing English even though he likes to read and is a very good writer. His parents believe that he tries very hard when he is experiencing success and the esteem of teachers, and shuts down when he is not doing well.

In Their Own Words
Students with LBLD Talk about School

My best teacher really was able to show me how to become a good writer and public speaker. Public speaking is a part of what I want to do in life and he gave me the confidence to push myself in so many areas I didn't think were possible.

Elizabeth, high school student

The best teacher I have had is from sixth grade because she helped me get over my fear of talking in front of people. She made me feel confident in my presentations and myself.

Kamara, high school student

It is no longer embarrassing to contribute in a group conversation. I am not afraid to ask questions or be unsure of something. Instead of being made fun of, I am supported. When I speak in a group now I am more confident and am willing to give my opinion.

Theo, high school student

I want students to engage the way a clutch on a car gets engaged: an engine can be running, making appropriate noises, burning fuel and creating exhaust fumes, but unless the clutch is engaged, nothing moves. It's all sound and smoke, and nobody gets anywhere.
- Robert L. Fried, The Passionate Teacher: A Practical Guide

WHAT TO DO

Include Students in the Learning Process

Landmark's sixth teaching principle calls us to include students in the learning process. We contribute to their academic success when we help them understand that people learn in different ways and guide them to identify their own learning style. Additionally, we enhance their motivation when we invite students to participate in planning how they will learn and how they will demonstrate their learning.

Students are not passive receptacles to fill with information. They come to class with their own frames of reference. Their unique experiences and knowledge affect them as learners and should be taken into account. As much as possible, teachers should accept student input on the learning experience and engage with what they say. This does not mean opening up a free-for-all discussion about the pros and cons of a lesson or course. It means creating an environment that guides constructive collaboration and fosters communication about how to enhance each student's learning experience. This may be done both individually and as a group.

Taking time prior to a new lesson or unit to overview the topics, frame essential questions to guide instruction, and set goals for learning is both a responsible teaching practice and an opportunity for collaboration. Likewise, making time at the end of a lesson or unit to reflect on the learning experience helps students consolidate new skills, information, and ideas and provides feedback to the teacher about what the next instructional steps might be.

Including students in assessing their own progress by reviewing assessment results and comparing them to previously established goals and objectives is one helpful way to empower students to participate fully in "grading," which is a commonly alienating experience for them, particularly those who rarely receive "good" grades. In addition, creating and improvising opportunities to involve students in the learning process helps them become more self-aware about how they learn and perform best, how certain strategies and skills benefit them, and what role their behavior plays in their success. These types of activities can increase self-efficacy (a core element of academic proficiency) as well as help teachers gain a clearer understanding of how best to support and enhance their students' learning.

When students are fully and authentically included in the learning process, their motivation and effort commonly increase. In short, an included student often becomes an invested student who is eager to exert effort to learn and perform.

Online Resource Available

Include Students in the Learning Process

These materials are available online for printing or customizing at www.landmarkoutreach.org/ef-resources. When you open this page, enter the username **(foundations)** and the password **(OUTREACH)**.

Motivation Questionnaire
For Younger Students

Name: _____ **Date:** _____

My 3 Favorite Activities In School

ACTIVITY	REASON I LIKE IT

My 3 Favorite Activities Outside of School

ACTIVITY	REASON I LIKE IT

How My Favorite Activities Make Me Feel (Write or Draw A Picture)

When I do my favorite activities, this is what my emotional feelings are:

I feel these emotions in my body like this:

MOTIVATION QUESTIONNAIRE

When I Don't Want to Do Something in School	
EXAMPLE	**REASON I DON'T FEEL LIKE DOING IT**

When I Don't Want to Do Something Outside of School	
EXAMPLE	**REASON I DON'T FEEL LIKE DOING IT**

How Activities I Don't Like Make Me Feel (Write or Draw A Picture)

When I have to do activities I don't like, this is what my emotional feelings are:

I feel these emotions in my body like this:

This is what I do when I don't feel like doing something:

Motivation Questionnaire
For Older Students

Name: _____ **Date:** _____

3 Academic Activities/Tasks I Generally Enjoy

ACTIVITY	REASON(S) I ENJOY IT

3 Activities/Tasks Outside of School I Generally Enjoy

ACTIVITY	REASON(S) I ENJOY IT

3 Academic Activities/Tasks I DO NOT Enjoy

ACTIVITY	REASON(S) I DO NOT ENJOY IT

3 Activities/Tasks Outside of School I DO NOT Enjoy

ACTIVITY	REASON(S) I DO NOT IT

Reflect Mindfully: How Do Activities/Tasks Make Me Feel

What emotions do you associate with activities/tasks you **enjoy**?	
What do these emotions feel like in your body? (e.g., lightness, alertness, smiling, etc.)	
What emotions do you associate with activities/tasks you **do not enjoy**?	
What do these emotions feel like in your body? (e.g., nausea, blankness, tightness in chest, etc.)	

MOTIVATION QUESTIONNAIRE

MOTIVATION QUESTIONNAIRE

Motivation Questionnaire for Older Students (Continued)

Our human needs range from basic survival needs to creativity and altruism, according to Abraham Maslow, a well-known psychologist. Maslow described these needs as a hierarchy in which the basic needs must be met before we could have the motivation and effort to meet higher level needs.

In this part of the motivation questionnaire, you will rate yourself on 26 items that may help you identify areas of need in your own life that can influence your motivation and effort. After you have completed the questionnaire, you can fill out the graphic organizer on the following page, and reflect on any ideas you have about motivation and effort.

Rate yourself on how often each statement is true for you by putting an x in the appropriate box.

	Never	Some of the time	Often	Almost Always
1) I have a place to live.				
2) I have enough food and water.				
3) I feel physically comfortable.				
4) I feel safe in my home.				
5) I feel safe at school.				
6) I feel safe in my neighborhood.				
7) I have people in my life who help me when needed.				
8) My home life is predictable and secure.				
9) I have a quiet and clean place to do my work.				
10) I know what my responsibilities are at home and school.				
11) I know how to do what I am supposed to do.				
12) I feel confident that I can meet my responsibilities successfully.				
13) I feel that others care about/love me.				
14) I feel that others care about my work.				
15) I have at least one close friend.				
16) My successes are acknowledged at school.				

Motivation Questionnaire for Older Students (Continued)				
17) My successes are acknowledged at home.				
18) I feel I have strengths and talents.				
19) I am curious, and I like to learn about new things.				
20) I like to make connections between the many things I see, or hear, or learn about.				
21) I need to understand things.				
22) I like to be creative and am often inspired by the creativity of others.				
23) I know what I need in order to feel happy and fulfilled in my life.				
24) I get a lot of satisfaction from doing well on something that is important to me.				
25) I feel that my activities and tasks have relevance to my life.				
26) I feel my activities and tasks are contributing something to others.				

Maslow's Hierarchy of Needs is shown here, with physiological needs at the bottom (the most basic needs). Notice that the "need to know and understand" (a need often filled by school) is fairly high in the hierarchy.

Are you motivated to exert the effort to fill this need? Why or why not? If you have difficulties with motivation and effort in any area of your life, take some time now to reflect upon what might be getting in your way. You may write on the back of this sheet. Consider paying particular attention to the items you rated as "Never" or "Some of the Time."

Please talk to a teacher or counselor if you experience any strong emotions during this activity.

Maslow's Hierarchy	
Needs Hierarchy	Question Alignment
Transcendence	26
Self-Actualization	23-25
Aesthetic	22
Know and Understand	19-21
Esteem	16-18
Belongingness and Love	13-15
Safety	4-12
Physiological	1-3

MOTIVATION QUESTIONNAIRE

Landmark's Sixth Teaching Principle™

INCLUDE STUDENTS IN THE LEARNING PROCESS

Students are not passive receptacles to fill with information. They come to class with their own frames of reference. Their unique experiences and knowledge affect them as learners and should be taken into account. Therefore, during every exercise, teachers should accept student input as much as possible. They should justify assignments, accept suggestions, solicit ideas, and provide ample time for students to share ideas. Teachers should include students in assessing their own progress by reviewing test results, written reports, and educational plans. Creating and improvising opportunities to involve students in the learning process allows students to become aware of how they learn and why certain skills benefit them. As a result, students are motivated and more likely to apply those skills when working independently. In short, an included student becomes an invested student who is eager to learn.

Many students assume there's a "normal" way to learn and study. They don't know that people use many different approaches to gain understanding and demonstrate what they have learned. Helping students understand their learning process is one of the most important steps we can take as teachers. So often, we teach our students the way we ourselves learn best. In doing so, we may be missing many opportunities to empower their learning.

Essential to being a good student – *and* to good teaching – is awareness of our individual preferences for thinking and learning. These preferences are far more complex than the basic understanding of learning styles that includes only visual, auditory, and kinesthetic.

Formative assessment for learning is a phrase commonly associated with including students in the learning process. Pared down to its basics, formative assessment asks us to assess students *while* they are learning, rather than waiting until afterward, as summative assessment does. Why? Ongoing assessment such as this keeps students and teachers focused on the learning objectives and gives them clear evidence of where their strengths and needs lie before it's too late to do anything differently. Formative assessment for learning necessitates more teacher-student interaction than is commonly found in a traditional classroom. It also happens to be a powerful approach to ensuring success for students with learning disabilities.

GOAL:
Work *with* students collaboratively to define clear learning objectives for lessons/units and plans for how students will demonstrate their learning.

INCLUDE STUDENTS IN THE LEARNING PROCESS

What to Do	Why to Do It	How-To Suggestions
Engage & Observe Plan in-class activities that engage students with the content and force them to interact with language.	Allows you to document your observations of individual students' strengths and needs relative to the learning objectives.	Try: debates; simulations; group projects; collaborative note-taking; student-led discussions; and games.
Feedback Give & Take Provide students with daily specific feedback about what they are doing well and what they need to do next so they can achieve the learning objectives.	Offers you the opportunity to answer specific questions and receive feedback from students about what they need in order to be more successful.	Accomplish this as you observe and interact with each student while they engage in class activities.
Confer Frequently Meet briefly with each student throughout the unit to discuss their progress toward demonstrating mastery of learning objectives, and suggest needed steps.	Provides an opportunity to document student progress in writing, and makes sure each student has a clear focus for his or her efforts.	If you're prepared and you keep your eye on the clock, 2 minutes per student should suffice. Confer 1x per week if possible, especially for longer units.
Design Unit Assessments Ensure that summative assessments actually measure the knowledge and skills you've targeted in the learning objectives.	Encourages you to design your assessments prior to teaching the unit so that you can focus on the essentials in your teaching, and test on what you've taught.	Organize assessments according to key knowledge areas and key skill areas you've covered in class. Rubrics can work well for this.
Teach Self-Evaluation Teach students how to analyze their performance on summative assessments and set goals for future learning activities.	Empowers students to assess their own performance with a teacher-like eye. Self-evaluation, and goal-setting are critical executive skills that can be taught.	Try: reflections; portfolio review sheets; test analysis sheets; and rubrics.

INCLUDE STUDENTS IN THE LEARNING PROCESS

INCLUDE STUDENTS IN THE LEARNING PROCESS

CLASS WRAP-UP STRATEGY

NAME: _____   DATE: _____

Take A Closer Look! Class Wrap-Up

What study skill(s) did we focus on today? Put a check next to the skills focused on in class.

Organization	Summarizing
Vocabulary development	Making Inferences
Pre-reading text	Generating questions
Locating the **main idea**	Highlighting
Locating the **details**	Preparing for tests
Textbook Skills	Using materials (text, notes & vocabulary cards)
Two Column Note-taking	Other:

What was the most important *concept* covered today?

_____

_____

What skill(s) or concept(s) do you want to *review/practice* again?

_____

_____

Dierdre Mulligan, Landmark Elementary Middle School, created the reflective activity on this page and the top of the next page. The sheet here is very closely adapted from the one she uses in her classroom (which includes both the "Take a Closer Look!" and the "Self-Ratings." It was first published in Landmark Outreach's free e-resource, *Spotlight on Language-Based Teaching*.

CLASS WRAP-UP STRATEGY

NAME: _____ **DATE:** _____

Self-Ratings: Circle Your Rating

	Needs Improvement	Satisfactory	Excellent
Homework Effort	1	2	3
Classwork Effort	1	2	3
Participation	1	2	3
Behavior	1	2	3

What could you do to increase your ratings tomorrow?

_____

_____

CLASS WRAP-UP STRATEGY

Exit Slip

Today I learned:

I need to practice more on:

I'm still wondering about:

INCLUDE STUDENTS IN THE LEARNING PROCESS

NOTES

Chapter 4
Executive Function and Academic Proficiency

What to Know

Executive function coordinates cognitive and psychological processes, as described in the previous chapters. These processes are the foundation for academic proficiency, which involves three interrelated areas: language and literacy skills, learning and study skills, and self-efficacy (see figure 1 in chapter 1). The development of all three areas relies on the dynamic interaction between students and the teachers who provide responsive instruction.

What and how we teach should be driven by what students know (their learning) and what they can do in different contexts (their performance or demonstration of learning). In other words, we must start where students are now. This is easier said than done. Understanding where students are now requires close observation, sensitive formative assessment, and a commitment to creating the time and venue to dialogue with individual students about their learning and performance experience. This shared understanding between each student and teacher can guide goal-setting as well as the specific feedback we give to students, our written reports, and parent conferences.

Effective learning and performance depends upon not only a student's unique neurobiological makeup but also the environment in which he or she is learning. Each of the areas of academic proficiency summarized here can be nurtured and empowered by skilled educators. None of us are superhuman; we can't expect that we alone are responsible to help students resolve all their academic struggles. We can guide them toward proficiency by modeling

> Students need explicit and individualized instruction to ensure that their listening, speaking, reading, and writing skills are sufficiently developed to match the complexity of the content they are expected to master.

and practicing attitudes and behaviors from which they can learn. One step in this process is recognizing the discrete but interrelated areas of academic proficiency. Another is evaluating where our students are now, where we would like them to be, and what we can do to help them get there.

Language and Literacy Skills

Language and literacy skills are essential to academic competence. Language skills—listening, speaking, reading, and writing—develop and are used interdependently, yet current educational conversations about literacy generally focus only on the written word—reading and writing. Students' academic success greatly depends on the depth and breadth of their oral as well as their written language skills.

Students speak, read, and write at varying levels of sophistication. Many need explicit and individualized instruction to ensure that their listening, speaking, reading, and writing skills are sufficiently developed to match the complexity of the content they are expected to master. This is called basic literacy. It is a foundation of the higher levels of literacy students are expected to demonstrate starting around fourth grade. Most students also require explicit instruction and guidance to learn to speak and write in the form of each academic discipline. This is called disciplinary literacy.

Basic Literacy

Often, literacy instruction is considered to encompass only reading and writing skills. However, those skills develop in direct relation to listening and speaking skills. Students' reading fluency develops not only from automatizing the "code" (the relation between symbols on the page and oral language that may occur when decoding or encoding), but also from their fund of semantic knowledge (vocabulary) and syntactic and discourse knowledge (structures of language beyond the single word level). These areas of knowledge enable students to reclassify what they read and hear into declarative memory and to reconstruct what they have learned so they may communicate it through speaking or writing. Comprehension is constructed relative to students' oral and written language knowledge.

Comprehension—the goal of communication—requires that student's interact with language using multiple modalities. In the words of one colleague from Landmark Outreach: "Students need to touch language." They need not only to listen and read, but also to speak and write. Basic literacy instruction should aim to develop both oral and written language skills using a multisensory approach.

> Comprehension—the goal of communication—requires that student's interact with language ..."Students need to touch language."

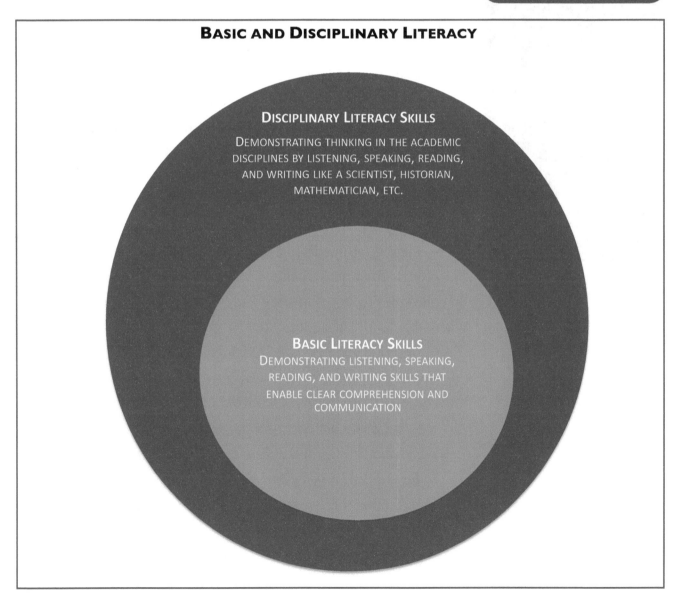

BASIC AND DISCIPLINARY LITERACY

DISCIPLINARY LITERACY SKILLS

DEMONSTRATING THINKING IN THE ACADEMIC DISCIPLINES BY LISTENING, SPEAKING, READING, AND WRITING LIKE A SCIENTIST, HISTORIAN, MATHEMATICIAN, ETC.

BASIC LITERACY SKILLS
DEMONSTRATING LISTENING, SPEAKING, READING, AND WRITING SKILLS THAT ENABLE CLEAR COMPREHENSION AND COMMUNICATION

Figure 10. Basic and disciplinary literacy.

> Only with keen observation of the learning process, sensitive formative assessment, and clear communication with our students will we be able to offer interventions that bridge the disconnect in skills and guide students to becoming truly proficient with language and literacy.

Disciplinary Literacy

While basic literacy skills remain the same across academic disciplines, disciplinary literacy skills enable students to listen, speak, read, and write from a variety of perspectives. For instance, scientists approach knowledge and ideas differently from historians, and the conventions for how they communicate are different. An historical essay looks very different from a lab report. Starting as early as third or fourth grade, students begin learning the scientific method, for example. This process of thinking about information and writing about interactions with that information is quite different from reading or writing a story, or researching and writing about an historical event. The extent of students' facility with basic literacy skills, and the explicit instruction and practice their teachers provide for them on the conventions of each academic discipline will determine the extent to which they can engage in disciplinary literacy. Too often, students are expected to demonstrate disciplinary literacy skills that far outpace the level of their basic literacy skills. This disconnect between where students are now and where their teachers expect them to be causes many difficulties.

Michael Mascolo, college professor and founding editor of the peer-reviewed online discussion group, *Pedagogy and the Human Sciences*, is frustrated by this disconnect. In a recent post, he called on colleagues to stop lecturing and "find ways to engage students where they are." He writes:

> At one point, I decided to change what I was doing. I decided I wanted to take what people now call "learning outcomes" seriously. What would happen if we really took seriously our ideals about what we want students to learn and who we want them to be? We want our students to be critical thinkers and all of that. They are so far from that. Given where they are right now, I'd settle for "thinkers", let alone critical thinkers.
>
> Why? Because our students tend not to have the most basic of skills. We lament their incapacity to write. But there is something even more important: Most students

cannot read. Sure, they can move their eyes across the page, decode the words—but a plurality of college students have no real way of reading for comprehension! Why is this? (Mascolo, 2014).

Only with keen observation of the learning process, sensitive formative assessment, and clear communication with our students will we be able to offer interventions that bridge the disconnect in skills and guide students to becoming truly proficient with language and literacy.

> Teaching students skills is one concrete and straightforward way we can empower their executive function.

Learning and Study Skills

To succeed in school, students must develop strong learning and study skills as well as strong language and literacy skills. To do well on a test, for example, students must read, listen to, comprehend, process, remember, and express knowledge and ideas about the content. Their ability to read and listen strategically, take organized notes, keep track of books and papers, use time productively, and engage in learning and study strategies appropriate to the subject matter greatly enhances the likelihood that they will succeed.

Effective implementation of learning and study skills requires behavioral and attitudinal self-regulation—what many see as lying at the core of executive function. It also requires explicit instruction and guided practice in specific strategies to manage materials, time, and language. Teaching students strategies is one concrete and straightforward way we can empower their executive function. Over time, we can guide them to combine their discrete strategies into automatic skilled routines that foster successful learning and prevent them from becoming overwhelmed by the expectations of their academic work.

Self-Efficacy

As students develop language, literacy, learning, and study skills, they must also develop attitudes that empower them to use

> Students with higher self-efficacy tend to participate more readily, work harder, pursue challenging goals, spend much effort toward fulfilling identified goals, and persist longer in the face of difficulty. (Hsieh, Sullivan, and Guerra, 2007)

their skills. Academic proficiency requires self-efficacy. Self-efficacy is the feeling of confidence that our behavior will directly lead to achieving a goal. Without it, students are likely to give up in the face of a challenge and ascribe any success they achieve to luck rather than their own skills and efforts.

SELF-EFFICACY

Self-efficacy grows as students develop three skill sets: self-awareness, self-assessment, and self-advocacy.

Develop self-awareness skills by tuning in to what they are feeling and doing, and ascribing their successes and failures accurately so they may set goals and plan for future successes.

Develop self-assessment skills by learning to recognize and acknowledge their personal and academic strengths and vulnerabilities/needs.

Develop self-advocacy skills by practicing the communication skills required to negotiate for what they need, and flexibly seeking out creative alternatives when required.

According to Hsieh, Sullivan, and Guerra (2007):

Students with higher self-efficacy tend to participate more readily, work harder, pursue challenging goals, spend much effort toward fulfilling identified goals, and persist longer in the face of difficulty.... Students not only need to have the ability and acquire the skills to perform successfully on academic tasks, they also need to develop a strong belief that they are capable of completing tasks successfully. (p. 457)

Students begin to understand the connection (or disconnection) between their actions and their grades when we:

1. explicitly teach them specific strategies
2. engage them in observation and dialogue about how they use the strategies
3. reflect with them about how their behaviors impact their performance in class and on assessments

Such teaching develops students' executive function and self-efficacy. Many students need help seeing, understanding, and evaluating their role in their academic success.

Academic Success

Teachers, parents, and students themselves know that success breeds success. It is essential, then, that students learn the strategies to develop the skills they need to succeed in school. Some students develop language and literacy skills, learning and study skills, and self-efficacy with little guidance. Most, however, are learning apprentices who require mentoring from their teachers—explicit instruction, continuous guided practice, and feedback—to make sense of and communicate about the vast array of information and ideas they encounter each day.

This type of mentoring supports the development of academic proficiency and executive function. Howard Gardner (2007), well known for his theory of multiple intelligences, captures the relationship succinctly:

> *Drawing on long-established categories of human psychology, we construe executive function as the integration of three parameters: hill—the establishment of a clear goal; skill—the requisite abilities and techniques for attaining that goal; and will—the volition to begin and persevere until the goal has been reached. (p. 20)*

Teachers can empower all students to identify and understand the hill, mentor them as they develop the skill to climb it, and partner with them as they strengthen their will to succeed.

> Most students are learning apprentices who require mentoring from their teachers—explicit instruction, continuous guided practice, and feedback—to make sense of and communicate about the vast array of information and ideas they encounter each day.

STUDENT PROFILES

STUDENT PROFILES

The student profiles section of each chapter introduces different facets of five students: Enrique, Petra, Adonis, Jonelsi, and Nathan. Each experiences difficulties in school that teachers must analyze and address. The profiles are composites of several actual students whose names have been changed here.

Students have unique learning profiles that reflect their educational experience from the past and influence their current experience in school. Elements of their profiles include their learning, thinking, and personality styles; their emotion, motivation, and effort; and their particular areas of need for language acquisition and use. All students who struggle in school - particularly those with LBLD - benefit from structured, multisensory, skills-based instruction. Each requires individualized instruction targeted at his or her specific needs. The student profiles in this book are included to encourage teachers' thinking about students in their own classes.

Model and Microunit

As you read about interventions for each student, keep in mind the following questions:

FROM WHAT YOU'VE READ ABOUT THE STUDENT SO FAR, DO YOU THINK THIS INTERVENTION WILL ADDRESS HIS OR HER NEEDS?

WHAT OTHER INTERVENTIONS MIGHT BE APPROPRIATE FOR THIS STUDENT?

IF THIS WERE YOUR STUDENT, WHAT WOULD YOU DO TO PROVIDE SUPPORT?

Also think about your own students:

WHICH OF YOUR STUDENTS MIGHT BE STRUGGLING WITH ISSUES RELATED TO LANGUAGE & LITERACY SKILLS, LEARNING & STUDY SKILLS, OR SELF-EFFICACY?

WHAT EVIDENCE OR EXAMPLES LEAD YOU TO THINK THEY ARE STRUGGLING IN ONE OR MORE OF THESE AREAS?

WHAT RESOURCES ARE AVAILABLE TO YOU TO SUPPORT YOUR STUDENTS?

Enrique, Grade 3

ENRIQUE has recently been meeting with a high school student named Jared who is a volunteer mentor for students with learning disabilities and differences. Jared also has a learning disability, and is passionate about wanting to support younger students because he remembers how difficult it was for him. Once each week they play basketball together and talk about what it's like to be in school when you have an LD. Enrique's mother has also been reading to him about learning differences so that he understands why working on reading in a separate group will be helpful to him. Enrique's teacher has agreed to return students' work in a more private way, and she and Enrique have set up a system together so that his corrections are manageable. In addition, his recent reading scores show that he is making rapid gains as a result of his new intensive reading program. Enrique is very enthusiastic about his time with Jared, his physical complaints have decreased significantly, and he now feels less afraid to talk to his teacher when he is frustrated.

Petra, Grade 5

PETRA and her father met with the school counselor to discuss how best to support Petra and her family. While her father was initially upset, he agreed that additional support was needed. With a variety of people helping to plan, Petra's younger brothers now attend an after-school program, and Petra has joined several clubs. She continues to attend the school's social skills group. In addition, she attends weekly counseling at the city's nearby trauma center. The school has arranged for all three children to be provided with breakfast and lunch daily, and volunteers from Petra's church are providing dinners for the family twice per week. Petra's teachers report that they see a difference in her—a few smiles, more alertness and engagement. They are hopeful that as Petra begins to heal from trauma she will make more friends and be better able to complete her work.

Adonis, Grade 7

ADONIS has continued to demonstrate behavior issues, and his teachers and counselors are working with him on a daily basis to support him. They have observed that most of the behaviors now occur in the cafeteria and in the gym, when Adonis is with friends who are not part of the language-based classroom. In class, his teachers observe that Adonis has made friends, seems better able to focus on his work, and exhibits pride in selecting pieces for his portfolio. Weekly assessments show his reading and writing fluency are improving at the desired pace, and he complains about the classwork and homework with less frequency.

STUDENT PROFILES

STUDENT PROFILES

JONELSI is now on a trial of medication for ADHD and she reports feeling much better able to concentrate on her work and follow conversations. She is scheduled for a speech-language evaluation to assess further the language processing deficits that showed up in her neuropsychological evaluation. In addition, she sees a counselor once per week to build her emotional health. At the counselor's recommendation, Jonelsi has also been participating in the Tai Chi club after school, and has bartered free babysitting in exchange for yoga classes from a neighbor who owns a local studio. She reports that both these activities make her feel calmer and more confident. She is hoping to re-join the school band in 10th grade. Jonelsi continues to struggle in class and finds it very difficult to ask the teacher or another student for assistance even when she knows she needs it, and she continues to work on inhibiting her impulsive comments and behaviors that so frequently get her into trouble.

Jonelsi, Grade 9

NATHAN's parents now require him to sit in the living room to do his work and to report to them what is due and what progress he has made. Nathan is quite angry about it but has agreed to do it to avoid losing the privilege of driving the car. The situation is less than ideal, and his parents soon realize that they do not know whether Nathan is telling the truth about his assignments and progress. As things continue to worsen, the guidance counselor sets up a weekly check-in with Nathan. Before the meeting, the counselor gathers updates from Nathan's teachers, then discusses the situation with Nathan, helps him make a plan for completion, and requires Nathan to email him when the work is complete. The guidance counselor stays in weekly contact with Nathan's parents as well. This record of communication provides a sort of journal that the guidance counselor uses to help Nathan see his academic avoidance patterns. In addition, the guidance counselor is working with Nathan on developing the self-advocacy skills to talk to his teachers about what he needs.

Nathan, Grade 11

In Their Own Words
Students with LBLD Talk about School

Participating helps me learn because saying it out loud helps me understand what I am thinking or talking about.

Darius, elementary school student

(My best teacher) helped me structure and figure out how to write a successful essay. I can now be proud of my essays.

Gideon, middle school student

What's challenging for me in school, is when I am called on when my hand is not raised. This makes me stiffen up, become anxious and ultimately shutdown.

Eliza, middle school student

My best success is finding out that I enjoy writing, and am starting to get fairly good at it. I was empowered by this when a published author wrote to me and told me that I had a good "Turn of Phrase."

Michelina, high school student

Just think about what you know today. You read. You write. You work with numbers. You solve problems. We take all these things for granted. But of course you haven't always read. You haven't always known how to write. You weren't born knowing how to subtract 199 from 600. Someone showed you. There was a moment when you moved from not knowing to knowing, from not understanding to understanding. That's why I became a teacher.

\- Phillip Done, teacher and author

WHAT TO DO

Provide Models, Microunit, and Guide Practice

From infancy onward, we need models to learn new skills. Infants' babbling mirrors the sounds of caregivers and lays the foundation that enables them to develop spoken language. Children learn by watching models and mimicking—to dress themselves, show manners, and swing on a swing set, for example.

In fact, throughout our lives we depend upon observation of models to help us learn. We follow diagrams to learn how to repair a leaking faucet and watch how a dog trainer gets our pet to respond to commands. These types of models help us learn efficiently and effectively.

Oddly enough, as students move through school, they often lack access to models for academic skills. Though we ask students to "take notes," we don't always show them what good notes look like, or teach them how to do it. The same might be said for comprehending reading material, writing essays, or studying for tests. Some teachers may assume students already possess a skill, so they don't model or teach it. Others may feel that providing models inhibits creativity or prevents students from learning to do something independently. Though most students muddle through, they could be far more successful if they had models and explicit instruction to guide them. Provide Models is one of Landmark's Six Teaching Principles™.

Imagine attending a pottery class in which the instructor holds up a beautifully glazed teapot as a project model and provides a history of ceramic kitchenware. If the teacher's next step is telling the class to get started on a teapot of their own—due in a week— the results may be a disappointment to all. Instead, if the teacher chunked the project into sequential steps, modeled each step, and provided guidance along the way, many more students would sustain their efforts and find success. The model teapot, and the models of each step to make it do not inhibit creativity or prevent students from learning how to craft a pot. Instead, they empower students to persist through a complex process and achieve the goal.

We can't stop there. Once students have a model of what their work ought to look like, they need a road map and guided practice to achieve the goal. Microuniting is the term Landmark School uses when we refer to breaking a task into small parts that can be completed sequentially. Microunit and Structure Tasks is one of Landmark's Six Teaching Principles™. Microuniting prevents students from becoming overwhelmed by complex tasks such as writing a paper, constructing a project, or studying for a test. When we provide models, microunit and structure the discrete tasks involved, and provide guided instruction and practice as students are learning, we greatly decrease their anxiety and increase their potential to achieve success.

This section begins with a brief overview of the Gradual Release of Responsibility Model. So named by Pearson and Gallagher in 1983, the model is based upon the work of Lev Vygotsky, a developmental psychologist. It is intended to guide our instructional planning in order to increase students' active engagement with learning and foster their independence through an apprenticeship/mentoring model. The graphic representation of the model on the next page is adapted from one put forward by Doug Fisher and Nancy Fry (2008) in their book, *Better Learning Through Structured Teaching: A Framework for the Gradual Release of Responsibility, 2nd Edition.*

Online Resource Available

Providing Models and Microuniting/Structuring Learning

The tips and handouts that follow can be used as is, or adjusted to meet your particular teaching needs. They are also available online for printing or customizing at www.landmarkoutreach.org/ef-resources. When you open this page, enter the username (**foundations**) and the password (**OUTREACH**). None of these resources should take the place of formal educational or psychological evaluations for students who need them.

THE GRADUAL RELEASE OF RESPONSIBILITY MODEL FOR CREATING ACTIVE AND INDEPENDENT LEARNERS

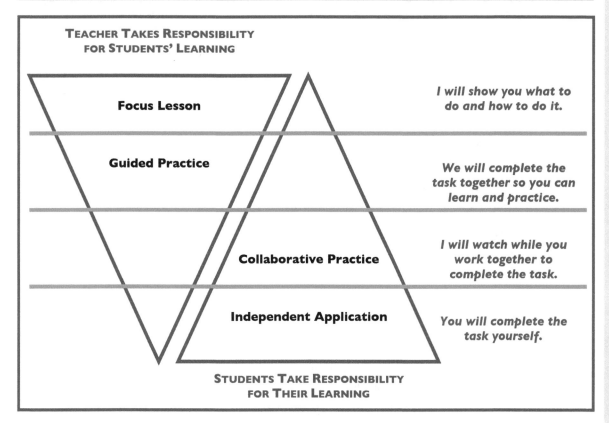

TEACHER TAKES RESPONSIBILITY FOR STUDENTS' LEARNING

Focus Lesson — *I will show you what to do and how to do it.*

Guided Practice — *We will complete the task together so you can learn and practice.*

Collaborative Practice — *I will watch while you work together to complete the task.*

Independent Application — *You will complete the task yourself.*

STUDENTS TAKE RESPONSIBILITY FOR THEIR LEARNING

GRADUAL RELEASE OF RESPONSIBILITY

The gradual release of responsibility model guides teachers to scaffold instruction so students learn effectively. Doug Fisher and Nancy Fry (2008) have written extensively on this model, and the graphic above is adapted from their presentations. In many classrooms, full teacher responsibility (the top of the triangle on the left) shifts quickly and directly to full student responsibility for learning (the bottom of the triangle on the right). While this instructional approach may work for some students some of the time, it disempowers and discourages most students, and often causes failure for students with learning disabilities. The middle sections of the triangle are essential components of instruction if we are committed to helping all our students become active and successful learners who can communicate their knowledge and ideas effectively.

As in a mentor/mentee or apprenticeship relationship, when a new task or skill is taught, the teacher begins by modeling the process while the students watch and ask questions. Once they understand their purpose, the scope of the work, and the outcomes expected, they are ready to begin working with close teacher guidance. As students develop and demonstrate the required skills, the teacher can gradually withdraw guidance while students help one another. Not until the end of the learning process are students expected to demonstrate knowledge and skills with full independence.

PROVIDE MODELS

7 Steps to Providing Models

PROVIDING MODELS IS SIMPLE, AND IMPORTANT.

Throughout our lives we depend upon observation of models to help us learn efficiently and effectively. Any adult who has attempted to master a new skill – knitting, pottery, boatbuilding or scuba diving, for example – knows the importance of having a patient and encouraging teacher as a guide. They provide step-by-step models and guide us as we fumble to master each challenge along the way. Great teachers and coaches are not only knowledgeable and skilled, they are also very good at chunking complex processes into doable tasks that help their students succeed.

So, how can we get better at using models in our classrooms? **Try the following 7 steps**, and pay attention to the differences in students' attitudes and performance.

	Planning steps
STEP 1	<u>IDENTIFY</u> a skill you expect students to demonstrate. Example Skill: Summarize the main ideas of an expository reading selection.
STEP 2	<u>ANALYZE</u> the components or steps of the skill, <u>list</u> them in sequence for yourself, and <u>PLAN</u> a way to model each step. Note that once you begin this process, you'll often identify pre-requisite sub-skills that will impact a student's ability to be successful. For instance, in the example that follows, the ability to identify main ideas is essential to successful summary-writing. Often it's necessary to backpedal and teach each sub-skill thoroughly prior to teaching a more complex skill such as summary writing.
STEP 3	<u>FIND OR CREATE MODELS</u> of each of the components identified in step 2 and a model of what the end–product should look like. In the example that follows, each step should have a model. For the "preview the reading selection" step, students might first look at and discuss a completed questionnaire about a given selection, then complete one of their own about a different selection. Additionally, there should be a model of the end-product, such as an example of a written summary of a text students have read.
	Instructional Steps
STEP 4	<u>INTRODUCE THE SKILL AND THE MODEL OF THE END-PRODUCT</u> to students, letting them know they will be learning the steps to master the skill.
STEP 5	<u>INTRODUCE THE MODEL OF THE FIRST STEP, SHOW STUDENTS HOW TO DO IT, AND WORK WITH THEM AS THEY PRACTICE</u>. Follow this process for each succeeding step (adding additional practice in each as needed) until all of the steps are complete.
STEP 6	<u>DISCUSS</u> with students the difficulties and successes they experienced along the way, and work with them to set goals for the next activity in which they'll use the skill.
STEP 7	<u>REPEAT</u> steps 1-6 for the next activity, and note that students gain skill as they practice.

Example: Steps & Strategies for Summarizing	
Steps	**Strategies**
Preview the reading selection	Examine the selection's length, structure, related illustrations, images, callout boxes, highlighted vocabulary, etc. Consider having students fill out a preview questionnaire.
Identify the topic	Look at the title and subtitles, and read a sentence or two at the beginning and end of the selection. Note the topic on the preview questionnaire.
Access prior knowledge about the topic	Identify any information about the topic or how it connects with other things learned in or outside of class. Brainstorm as a class, or have students brainstorm on their preview questionnaires.
Make predictions about the content's purpose	Consider the context for the selection and predict its purpose – e.g., a newspaper selection has a different purpose depending upon what section of the paper it's in; a textbook selection has a different purpose than a blog post. Note the purpose on the preview questionnaire.
Set a purpose for reading	For this activity, the purpose is to identify the main ideas in order to summarize the selection. The teacher can set a purpose for reading (e.g., You are to read this selection to find out about the process of photosynthesis), or the students can determine the purpose as a group.
Read the selection	Decode each word and sentence of the selection in order, from beginning to end. Read aloud or listen to it being read. (Students often skip the actual reading of the material, forging ahead instead to answer questions or complete the assignment.)
Identify the main ideas and their supporting evidence/examples	Generally, each paragraph or section of a text has a main idea that is explained or supported further with specific examples, facts, or other evidence. Underline or highlight each main idea.
Take two-column/Cornell notes	Write the topic of the reading selection at the top of the page, then write the main ideas in the left column, and supporting evidence/examples in the right column.
Write a topic sentence for the summary.	Write a sentence that gives the title, author, and topic of the selection.
Write a sentence about each main idea in the selection.	In the sequence in which they appear in the two-column/Cornell notes, paraphrase each main idea and write it in a sentence.

PROVIDE MODELS

PROVIDE MODELS

PREVIEWING QUESTIONNAIRE

Name: _____   Date: _____

Reference Information

Title of Text: _____

Author of Text: _____ Date of Text: _____

Preview

How long is what I have to read? _____ pages/paragraphs

How long will it take me to read it? _____minutes

How many illustrations/graphics are there? _____

Are there vocabulary words highlighted? _____

Are there questions at the end of the text? _____

Identify Topic

What is the topic of this text?

Access Prior Knowledge

Brainstorm of what I know about this topic.

How will this text connect with other things I'm learning in this class.

Text Purpose

What is the purpose of this text?

Set Purpose for Reading

Why am I reading this text?

Micro-Unit and Structure Tasks

STEP 1	**PLAN.** **DETERMINE THE SEQUENCE OF STEPS STUDENTS MUST PERFORM IN ORDER TO LEARN AND DEMONSTRATE LEARNING SUCCESSFULLY.** When we plan a lesson or generate an assignment, we can complete it ourselves before giving it to the students. This step, often skipped due to time, is an easy way to identify potential areas of confusion or difficulty for our students and to be aware of the subtasks involved in the learning activities.
STEP 2	**COMMUNICATE GOALS.** **SHARE WITH STUDENTS THE GOALS AND STEPS WE'VE IDENTIFIED IN STEP 1.** This makes goals clear to students and offers them a roadmap to get there. This step also serves to model for students how to break down a complex task for themselves. Eventually, we can invite students to participate in step 1 with us.
STEP 3	**TEACH AND PRACTICE.** **TEACH STUDENTS, STEP-BY-STEP, TO LEARN THE ESSENTIAL CONTENT AND APPLY THE ESSENTIAL SKILLS WE'VE IDENTIFIED.**
STEP 4	**ASSESS.** **MEASURE AND CELEBRATE OUR STUDENTS' SUCCESS (ALONG EACH STEP OF THE WAY).** Our students are encouraged to persevere, and we gain valuable information about which students need additional instruction and which students have demonstrated mastery.

Within Step 3:

Example Skill	Teach

Craft a Topic Sentence	• Examine and discuss model topic sentences.
	 • Identify topic sentences in paragraphs.
	 • Teach the basic formula for writing a topic sentence:
	     Topic (what you are writing about)
	     + controlling idea (the point you want to make about the topic)
	         Topic: lima beans
	         + controlling idea: are disgusting
	         Topic sentence: Lima beans are disgusting.
	 • As a class, practice generating topic sentences about familiar items and ideas **orally**.
	 • Practice **writing** topic sentences in small groups.
	 • Have students write a topic sentence independently.

MICROUNIT AND STRUCTURE

Micro-Unit and Structure Tasks

5-Step Writing Process

Giving the assignment, "write a paragraph" or "write an essay," is not enough for students with language-based learning disabilities. Most students will skip the very important pre-writing tasks that make writing a logical and thorough composition much easier. The steps of the process need to be explicitly taught, modeled, and practiced with guidance.

STEP 1	**BRAINSTORM** ABOUT THE TOPIC. List as many ideas and examples as you can *in no particular order*. • Productive brainstorming requires students to have enough background knowledge of a topic to produce language and ideas.
STEP 2	**ORGANIZE** YOUR IDEAS. Create an outline or graphic organizer that sequences the best ideas from your brainstorm. • If the assignment is an essay, categorize your brainstorm into subtopics for each paragraph of the essay. • Additionally, choose from your brainstorm or generate relevant information to support your sub-topics.
STEP 3	WRITE A **ROUGH DRAFT**. Using your outline or graphic organizer as a guide, write your paragraph or essay using complete sentences. *This draft does not have to be perfect, but should be complete.* • Many students with LBLD benefit from using paragraph templates that cue them to structure their discourse into paragraphs with topic sentences, supports, and concluding sentences.
STEP 4	**PROOFREAD** AND EDIT YOUR ROUGH DRAFT. Look for mistakes in word choice, grammar, spelling, organization, clarity, etc. • This stage is easier for students if the teacher provides a specific checklist of proofreading tasks to complete (underline your topic sentence, change 5 words to add more description, etc.).
STEP 5	MAKE CORRECTIONS TO CREATE A **FINAL DRAFT**. This final product should reflect all changes noted in the proofreading stage.

Micro-Unit and Structure the Basic Paragraph

Following are examples of a completed graphic organizer and a completed paragraph template (see steps 2 and 3). Students who are writing essays will need to use one of these for each of their body paragraphs. It should be noted that not all students need to complete both parts—some students will be able to generate paragraphs directly from the graphic organizer. Many students with LBLD, however, will benefit from the additional structure the paragraph template offers. As these students internalize the structure, they can be guided to apply it independently as they compose paragraphs from their graphic organizers.

Basic Paragraph 1: Graphic Organizer

topic: <u>schools</u>

controlling idea: <u>should be more responsible about paper</u>

supporting detail #1:

put recycling bins in the cafeteria

supporting detail #2:

save unused paper in binders and notebooks

supporting detail #3:

rule that all photocopies should be double-sided

MICRO-UNIT AND STRUCTURE TASKS

MICRO-UNIT AND STRUCTURE TASKS

Micro-Unit and Structure the Basic Paragraph

Students should use their completed graphic organizers to fill out the basic paragraph template. The ideas are the same as those on the graphic organizer, but the template requires complete sentences. It is important to note that many students must learn how-to write each element of a paragraph (topic sentence, supports, concluding sentence) in isolation prior to being asked to complete a graphic organizer and paragraph template.

1. To write the topic sentence, students combine their topic and controlling idea into a complete sentence. Some students may require additional structure and guidance to do this.
2. A basic paragraph template includes transition words as sentence starters. Students take the supporting details from their graphic organizers and write them in complete sentences that begin with the transition word. They may opt to re-order their supporting details as they complete the template.
3. The template includes space for a concluding sentence. Many students will require models and additional instruction and practice in order to learn how to write a concluding sentence.

Topic Sentence (combine topic and controlling idea):

Schools should be more responsible about paper use.

First, the school should put recycling bins in the cafeteria because the trash bins are filled with wasted paper.

Also, students should save any unused paper in their binders so that it does not go to waste.

Finally, the school should make a rule that all photocopies must be double-sided to cut paper use in half.

In conclusion, having school rules about paper use and recycling will ensure that everyone makes an effort to reduce, reuse, and recycle.

Basic Paragraph Organizer

topic: _____

controlling idea: _____

supporting detail #1:

supporting detail #2:

supporting detail #3:

NOTES

Chapter 5
Learning Styles, Differences, and Disabilities

WHAT TO KNOW

Consciously or not, each of us has preferences for how we absorb, process, and express information and ideas. We learn best via particular sensory modalities and under particular environmental conditions. We process information, communicate what we think, and interact with others in our own preferred ways. We also have unique, complex neural networks that influence our decisions about how we spend our time and how hard we work to meet a challenge. Perhaps most important, our preferences can shift, depending on the task and the environment.

Some of these individual differences are the result of neurobiological diversity—subtle differences in the way our brains work —while others develop in response to environmental factors. In other words, both our internal and external environments affect how successfully we can learn and demonstrate our learning.

Adults generally make personal and vocational choices that suit their preferences. Students do not have that latitude. They have little control over the courses they take, their teachers, or individual courses' academic level. They seldom have options for how they learn the course material or express their knowledge, and they generally do not have any control over how they are assessed and evaluated.

> The way we understand "normal" and "average" and the language we use to describe variations from those standards influence our perceptions of students who have difficulty learning in school.

Sociopolitical Factors in Learning Disability

School success is predicated on meeting predetermined standards. When a student cannot meet them, we generally investigate what is wrong with the student. Investigations often end in a diagnosis of some sort, and a label of "disability" or "disorder" so the student can receive "special" education. The way we understand "normal" and "average" and the language we use to describe variations from those standards influence our perceptions of students who have difficulty learning in school.

Shifting Thinking About Students' Academic Struggles

Many thoughtful individuals address the sociopolitical underpinnings of how we think, talk, and write about students who struggle and fail in school. One of the most powerful and informative conversations began in 2004 with Reid and Valle's "The Discursive Practice of Learning Disability: Implications for Instruction and Parent-School Relations" in the *Journal of Learning Disabilities*. This essay catalyzed a new discussion of learning disabilities.

Reid and Valle called for a shift in the way we understand difference and made the case for reexamining the way we understand learning disabilities. Their essay, and the responses to it, challenged the dominant paradigm of specific learning disability that continues to inform current research and practice in the field. This paradigm places the locus of a student's learning difficulty within the student without accounting for the learning environment. It does not recognize learning disability as a social construct (created in part, Reid and Valle argue, from the primacy of individualism in American culture) that cannot exist outside of school.

LEARNING DISABILITY IS A SOCIAL CONSTRUCT

"Learning and learning problems dwell in activities and cultural practices situated in the context of social relations rather than in the heads of individual students... [In other words,] LD is intelligible only in the context of schooling." (Dudley-Marling, 2004, pp. 482, 484)

Shifting Writing and Speaking About School Difficulty

Reid and Valle also addressed the discursive aspect of learning disability. Discourse refers to our use of language to communicate meaning. In order for language to be meaningful, it must follow an accepted set of structural rules as well as words for which there is general agreement about meaning. Discourse not only communicates but also creates meaning for ourselves and for the other(s) with whom we interact. When we speak or write about a topic, we reclassify what we knew about it previously; the same is true when we listen to or read another's discourse (see chapter 2 on reclassification in memory).

When we speak or write about individuals or groups of people, our discourse positions them in a particular way in our minds (and in the minds of people who listen to us or read what we wrote). Reid and Valle, paraphrasing the philosopher Michel Foucault (1972), remind us that:

> *A discourse is, then, both the system of rules that defines what can be said...and the instrument through which people become positioned, but not determined, within that discourse. (2004, p. 466)*

Reid and Valle ask us to examine two aspects of discourse about students struggling or failing in school: first, the words we use; second, the ways in which the students—and we ourselves—are shaped by these words.

> Reid and Valle (2004) ask us to examine two aspects of discourse about students struggling or failing in school: first, the words we use; second, the ways in which the students—and we ourselves—are shaped by these words.

DISCOURSE SHAPES THINKING: ONE EXAMPLE

Regular education (often called general education now) is an example of how discourse shapes thinking. A "regular" or "mainstream" classroom is one in which all students are expected to do similar work with about the same level of teacher support. The word implies that students outside this classroom, or working under different expectations within it, receive "irregular" education—a word with negative connotations. Though "special" education is the accepted term, it denotes not only difference but also carries profoundly negative connotations for students, parents and educators.

> That language alone can be powerful enough to position students in special education as abnormal or inferior is evidenced by the many hurtful epithets slyly communicated by regular education peers in the hallways, bathrooms, and on the playground.

That language alone can be powerful enough to position students in special education as abnormal or inferior is evidenced by the many hurtful epithets slyly communicated by regular education peers in the hallways, bathrooms, and on the playground. Many of us have even overheard fellow teachers refer to "sped-kids" with frustration or disdain. Such language puts the locus of difficulty within the student rather than within the curriculum and instruction.

What does all this have to do with a book about teaching students who struggle in school? Everything. It asks that we change the lens through which we view students who are having difficulty and our related responsibilities as educators.

About the term "learning disability," Reid and Valle (2004) write:

> *These human variations are often viewed as impairments. Our intention is to question conventional and naturalized ways of thinking about difference in order to bring greater balance to the intellectual grounding for understanding school failure and the decision-making that both emanates from that understanding and confirms it (Gallagher, 1999). Because what we think drives what we do (and vice versa), the way we frame difference has personal, material consequences for students and for the LD field as a whole. (p. 467)*

Connor (2005), who synthesized responses to Reid and Valle's article, notes that the authors call on us to reflect on our systems of belief. They ask us to question:

> *...the knowledge base on which our beliefs rest and, by doing so, compel us to ponder from where specific knowledge hails, how it was created, why it became enshrined as "truth," who is affected by this knowledge, and in what ways this knowledge affects the lives of all those connected to it. (pp. 159-160)*

Without denying the fact that some students struggle in school, Reid and Valle, and most of those who respond to them, awaken us to the notion that learning disabilities are socially constructed. As teachers, we can either contribute to the reification of that social construct by identifying the student as the locus of the problem and acting accordingly (such as by suggesting they try harder or get a tutor), or we can reexamine our beliefs and adjust our behavior so that more students learn successfully in our classes.

Disability Labels

Most people who have been categorized as learning-disabled take issue with the label. Though they do not deny their difficulties in school, they argue that the label falsely implies that they cannot learn. Jonathan Mooney, an honors graduate of Brown University and coauthor of *Learning Outside the Lines* (2000), did not learn to read until he was 12. He was diagnosed with learning disabilities and attention deficit/hyperactivity disorder (ADHD). Depressed, excluded, and ashamed, he suffered throughout his schooling. In a 2004 presentation, Mooney told Landmark High School students, "My problem in school wasn't a learning disability, it was a teaching disability." His comment points to the nature of the controversy about disability labels. They tacitly place difficulty within the individual without recognizing the impact of learning environments on the student's ability to learn.

While people with and without reading disabilities show neurological differences on brain imaging studies when they encounter written language, these differences can be mitigated with appropriate instruction. To a great extent, then, Mooney makes a legitimate argument: disabilities may be disabilities only because the student is not learning in an appropriate environment—that is, he or she is not receiving appropriate instruction.

Connor (2005) makes a similar point:

> *The reification of LD occurs because of schools and the highly controlled, specific academic demands placed on all children. In other words, when students are unable to meet predetermined standards due to the absence of certain abilities, the label is conferred. Furthermore, by*

> Most people who have been categorized as learning-disabled take issue with the label. Though they do not deny their difficulties in school, they argue that the label falsely implies that they cannot learn.

> The language we use to label people influences how we perceive and interact with them. It also influences how we perceive ourselves.

constantly stressing what students cannot do, as opposed to what they can do, school systems view children labeled LD through a lens of deficit. (p. 160)

Changing Language, Minds, and Actions

The language we use to label people influences how we perceive and interact with them. It also influences how we perceive ourselves. The development of sex-inclusive language, for example, both reflects and creates a changed perception of women in society. Using the word chair in place of chairman eliminates information about the individual's sex and reminds those who assume that men hold leadership positions that their assumption is false. The replacement of handicapped (which has derogatory roots) with universal access is another example. Universal access shifts the problem of accessibility away from the individual and toward the design of a building or environment. Changes in the language we use to describe students can have comparable effects on how they are perceived and treated.

On the forefront of educational thinking, terms like universal design for learning and differentiated instruction both reflect and create a gradual shift in perception about how individuals can and should learn. The tiered instructional model, also called response-to-intervention (RTI), is designed to ensure that students struggling in school are immediately identified and provided with instruction that meets their needs rather than allowed to fail and perhaps become labeled as learning-disabled.

TIERED INSTRUCTION

Mandated by the reauthorized Individuals with Disabilities Education Act (IDEA) in 2006, tiered instruction places responsibility for recognizing and remediating school difficulty on the environment rather than on the student and his or her family. While this shift in thinking, language, and action is a step toward addressing the issues discussed earlier, the fact remains that students whose skills do not increase quickly or effectively still end up being labeled "learning disabled."

When we shape curriculum and instruction to reflect an informed understanding of learning and thinking styles and personality and motivational profiles, more students learn successfully. While this truth is becoming more widely understood and accepted, individuals who do not meet the sociocultural criteria for "normal" or "average" continue to be categorized as disabled, disordered, dysfunctional, and so on. While the dialogical process of how changes in language alter perceptions is best left to linguists and cultural critics, educators should understand that the words we use to describe students who have difficulty learning the same way as most of their peers are controversial; they require reconsideration.

The Language of This Book

With now-obvious reservations, Landmark Outreach uses learning disability (LD) and language-based learning disability (LBLD) in our books. These terms continue to be the lingua franca of the educational world and special education law, and our goal above all is to provide knowledge and know-how to classroom teachers. We also use the terms learning style and learning difference. The definitions and distinctions among these terms are expanded upon below.

Learning Style

Learning style refers to a student's individual preferences for absorbing and expressing information and ideas. It is the set of preferences each of us brings to a learning experience. One view of this concept focuses on basic sensory perception; the other is more complex, as reflected in Howard Gardner's model for multiple intelligences (1983, 2006) and Robert Sternberg's concept of thinking styles and the triarchic theory of intelligence (1997, 2007). While Gardner's and Sternberg's work on learning and intelligence offers two examples among many, the links to curricular and instructional planning are particularly clear.

When we shape curriculum and instruction to reflect an informed understanding of learning and thinking styles and personality and motivational profiles, more students learn successfully. While this truth is becoming more widely understood and accepted, individuals who do not meet the sociocultural criteria for "normal" or "average" continue to be categorized as disabled, disordered, dysfunctional, and so on.

> Learning is far more complex than simply perceiving sensory stimuli. Our brains process and act upon those stimuli through a unique and intricate interplay of cognition, attention, memory, emotion, motivation, effort, personality, and executive function.

At the most basic level, our brains perceive stimuli through the five senses. Some people's sensory perception is stronger in one area than another, and most of us learn best when information and ideas are presented in a multisensory fashion. Novice teachers are often advised to let the wisdom of Confucius guide their planning: "I hear and I forget. I see and I remember. I do and I understand."

As chapters 2 and 3 discussed, however, learning is far more complex than simply perceiving sensory stimuli. Our brains process and act upon those stimuli through a unique and intricate interplay of attention, memory, emotion, motivation, effort, personality, and executive function. By taking some of these and other factors into consideration, Gardner's concept of multiple intelligences (often called learning styles in mass-media publications and Web sites) and Sternberg's work on thinking styles and successful intelligence provide rich explanations that we can use to enhance not only what we teach in our classrooms but also how we teach it. While the examples below do not capture the richness of either man's work, they illustrate how powerfully a good match between learning style and classroom environment can foster success.

LEARNING STYLES AND HOWARD GARDNER

While Howard Gardner's work on multiple intelligences has informed classrooms for decades, its oversimplification has prompted teachers to reject it. Teachers protest having to reshape their curriculum into song for those with musical intelligence or into numbers or patterns for those with mathematical intelligence, for example. Gardner's work in no way recommends that all curriculum be redesigned to match students' strengths. Rather, it highlights that human beings have many intelligences—more than those valued by the dominant culture or schools—and that wise educators recognize and use these strengths to engender dynamic learning environments and improved achievement.

Among the intelligences Gardner posits are an interpersonal intelligence and an intrapersonal intelligence. These intelligences represent one of the Big 5 in personality theory (in the Big 5 these are called extroversion and introversion). Those with interpersonal strengths tend to do well in classrooms oriented toward discussion, group projects, and cooperative learning. They also tend to be more comfortable asking questions, sharing opinions, and advocating for their and their friends' needs. Students with intrapersonal strengths, on the other hand, tend to do well in classrooms oriented toward personal reflection, individual projects, and self-guided learning. They may be quiet or shy in groups and have more difficulty speaking up. The point is, neither intelligence is better. Individuals with strengths in one or the other are simply different. In classrooms that are flexible enough, both kinds of students have opportunities to shine.

Sternberg's work on thinking styles and successful intelligence gives us insight into individuals' approaches to processing information and can profoundly shape the way we design curriculum and deliver instruction. Like Gardner, Sternberg does not articulate learning styles with the intention of prescribing how we should teach. His purpose is to enrich our understanding of how people learn and apply their knowledge and ideas. One example is his concept of legislative, executive, and judicial thinking styles in his

> Gardner's concept of multiple intelligences (often called learning styles in mass-media publications and Web sites) and Sternberg's work on thinking styles and successful intelligence provide rich explanations that we can use to enhance not only what we teach in our classrooms but also how we teach it.

THINKING STYLES AND ROBERT STERNBERG

Individual thinking styles influence how successfully we learn and interact in different environments. According to Robert Sternberg's thinking styles (1997), legislative thinkers like to make their own rules and do things their own way. They do well in classes where they can design experiments, choose research topics or books, and be creative in how they demonstrate their learning. Executive thinkers like to make and implement plans according to given guidelines. They often do well in traditional classrooms where they are told what to do and learn well while doing it. Judicial thinkers like to analyze and evaluate objects, people, and ideas. They do well in classrooms where critical thinking is valued.

> Students learn best—and become most successful and fulfilled — when their personal learning/ thinking styles match the learning environment. When students do not encounter such synchronicity, we challenge them to adapt. The insistence on locating learning problems—and their solutions— within the student displaces a responsibility that belongs to the learning environment.

theory of mental self-government. Individual self-government is like the United States government: the legislative branch decides what needs to be done, the executive branch makes sure it gets done, and the judicial branch decides whether legislation is grounded in and follows specific principles.

While all of us must develop strengths in each style, students and teachers with different preferences may find themselves in conflict. A teacher who is an executive thinker, for example, will find it very difficult to work with a student who is a judicial thinker unless the teacher understands how different approaches to thinking can cause conflict and can find ways to use the different styles to enhance their instruction and their students' learning. For example, the knowledgeable teacher who is an executive thinker might assign the judicial student the role of critiquing particular hypotheses, approaches, or interpretations.

Students learn best—and become most successful and fulfilled —when their personal learning/thinking styles match the learning environment. When students do not encounter such synchronicity, they must overcome environmental challenges to learning by adapting their learning behavior to the environment. The insistence on locating learning problems—and their solutions—within the student displaces a responsibility that belongs to the learning environment.

Learning Difference

All students who seem to have more potential than their school performance indicates—whether or not they meet diagnostic criteria for a learning disorder/disability—exhibit a learning difference. The environments in which they learn prevent them from achieving their full potential regardless of their efforts. They do not learn the material as well, and their performance suffers. A learning difference (mismatch between student and learning environment) can create a cycle of anxiety, frustration, and reduced self-esteem that exacerbates the initial difficulties. Sometimes minor accommodations can have a significant positive impact on these students' performance and academic self-concept, such as extra time on assignments or exams, extra help from the teacher, or exposure to content in an alternative form. Tiered instruction is intended to address some learning differences, beginning in the general education classroom and gradually intensifying levels of support until the student experiencing difficulty gains proficiency. When a student does not make effective progress, some form of diagnostic assessment is required to confirm that instruction is being appropriately targeted and delivered, and of sufficient duration.

> **EMPOWERING STUDENTS WITH LEARNING DIFFERENCES**
>
> Many students in our classrooms learn differently from the way we teach. We can empower them by deepening our understanding of learning diversity and increasing, by helping them understand and articulate how they learn best, and by including them – even the youngest – in the learning process. We collaborate with them to set learning goals and plan how best to achieve them.

Some students cannot adequately adapt when the learning environment does not match their learning style. Even with extraordinary effort, these students reap little in return.

Learning Disability

Some students cannot learn much at all when there is a mismatch between their learning environment and their learning style. Even with extraordinary effort, these students reap little in return. Their learning differences are so marked that they fall far behind their peers in developing academic proficiency. At some point in their lives, such students may be diagnosed with a learning disability/disorder.

EVALUATION AND DIAGNOSIS

Setting aside the controversy about disability labels, neuropsychological and speech-language evaluations, diagnoses, and recommendations for instruction continue to be of consummate importance for many students struggling in school. Thorough evaluations help explain what should be done to provide more effective instruction for a student who is struggling. Timely evaluation is especially pressing for students who have failed to make effective progress within a tiered instructional model. In a tiered instructional model, students who experience difficulty are

> A specific learning disorder (called specific learning disability in educational circles) describes individuals whose brains function so differently from most others that even though they have average-to-superior cognitive capacities, they cannot learn *the same way* most people do.

immediately provided with responsive instruction. Their progress is measured, and further instruction of different types or duration is provided until they demonstrate the skills they need to be successful in the general classroom. Among the goals of RTI are improved student achievement and earlier identification of students who require intervention.

Though the descriptions of a student's performance on testing can be confusing to parents and educators, evaluators' recommendations for appropriate instruction are usually understandable. Until all classroom teachers are knowledgeable about identifying learning differences and shaping curriculum and instruction to address them, these recommendations should be available for guidance. In addition, a diagnosis of a disability continues to be required by all states for students to be eligible for special education and to receive appropriate educational services.

DIAGNOSED LEARNING DISORDER

People with a learning disability have been diagnosed with or meet the diagnostic criteria for a specific learning disorder according to the *Diagnostic and Statistical Manual of Mental Disorders*, the American Psychiatric Association (APA) publication that guides physicians' and neuropsychologists' diagnoses. Individuals with a language-based learning disability (LBLD) are those whose difficulties specifically relate to the ways they perceive, process, and produce language (listening, speaking, reading, and writing).

From a neuropsychological point of view, a specific learning disorder (called specific learning disability in educational circles) describes individuals whose brains function so differently from most others that even though they have average-to-superior cognitive capacities, they cannot learn *the same way* most people do. Individuals diagnosed with reading disorders, for example, use a different part of their brains to approach written text than fluent readers. They can, however, learn to read fluently when given instruction that matches their learning style. This instruction must be delivered with fidelity by instructors trained to remediate reading difficulty, and must be of sufficient intensity and duration to ensure that the student is making effective progress toward reading proficiency.

In Their Own Words
Students with LBLD Talk about School

My school says they can teach kids who learn differently, but all they do is take you out of the room and put you with an inclusion specialist who teaches it the same way but just does it seventeen times until it is just drilled into you. It's awful.

John, middle school student

I value...when a teacher can do it—the ability to see when a student is struggling or not getting the material, and then to help in a constructive way so the student will understand the material.

Linda, high school student

The hardest thing I have ever done, to this day, is try to take notes by listening to my teacher. My ability to listen is so inexplicably awful, that well it's inexplicable. When I am in a social environment I don't have as much trouble. This is most likely because I'm more engaged in the conversation and am not learning something completely new.

Mel, high school student

Everybody is a genius. But if you judge a fish by its ability to climb a tree, it will live its whole life believing that it is stupid.

- Albert Einstein, physicist

Afterword

This book has aimed at introducing executive function and its foundational impact on learning in a straightforward and useful way for classroom teachers and other educators interested in understanding how people learn. The suggested teaching approaches and strategies at the end of chapters 1-4 provide a small array of ideas and models from which teachers can draw inspiration for enhancing their classroom instruction. The Recommended Resources section provides suggestions for how to learn more.

Many types of difficulties can interfere with students' academic progress; the recommendations for interventions that specialists make should be taken seriously. Keep in mind, however, that formal assessments of attention and executive function often fail to identify students with difficulties in these areas. Clinical interviews, parent and teacher observation and input, and students' self-reports tend to be far better indicators of the types of difficulties students have, and the circumstances when they are most likely to have them.

One of the most important things we can do as educators is interact in an attuned way with our students. To become teachers who can empower students to develop their knowledge and skills so they can be independent learners (the goal most of us have), we must choose to connect with our students as individuals—make our classrooms safe spaces for students to learn about not only the content, but also about themselves and others in the classroom community. Notice and talk with them about what they seem to be feeling and how they behave. Include them in the learning process so that we and they gain keener awareness of optimal conditions for successful learning and performance.

It is so easy to become overwhelmed by our students' many needs. No one classroom teacher can do everything. In the ideal world, there would be a magical transformation each of us could bring about; all our students' needs would be met, and they'd leave our classrooms as fully prepared as independent learners. Alas, the realities are a far cry from the ideal, and too many teachers give up or burn out as a result of feeling ineffective. The pressure on teachers to "do it all" may be internal or external, implicit or explicit, but it is always there because we can always do "better." In addition to teaching content and skills, we are expected and expect ourselves to coach students as they develop the collaborative and interpersonal skills, self-efficacy, self-regulation, and emotional resiliency that provide the foundation for their success in higher education, the workplace, and the 21st Century world. It's a tall order. This is why schools must build and strengthen teams of people who actively collaborate on many fronts to ensure that all students develop the capabilities they need to be successful in the next phases of their lives—whether this is a transition to the next grade, to college, or to the work world.

In the meantime, it's easy to forget that if we try to "fix" too many things at once or become rigid in our expectations or instructional approaches, we will never really empower our students—especially those who have learning differences or learning disabilities. So what should we do? Understand how people learn. Know our students. Collect a good-sized toolbox of strategies that meet particular needs. Give ourselves and our students the time and guidance to learn how to do things and practice until they become successful, or to learn how to start over using a different strategy. Be flexible in our instructional approaches. **And...start small...one strategy at a time. Observe students and try a strategy or two. Get their feedback on what works, and go from there!**

Most educators reading this book have all sorts of successful things happening in their classrooms. This book does not advocate changing what works. Instead, it offers a lens through which readers might understand some roadblocks to student success, and suggestions for approaches to get around them.

Landmark Outreach provides many resources to help teachers empower students' learning. Please visit our website at *www.landmarkoutreach.org*, and join our mailing list to receive our free e-resource, *Spotlight on Language-Based Teaching*.

Don't forget to visit this book's page on our site and leave your comments and questions! We do listen and value your ideas. We also regularly adjust our programming and publications in response to your feedback.

Glossary of Terms

ACADEMIC PROFICIENCY is the use and coordination of skills in order to demonstrate understanding of curriculum and perform at average or better levels on classroom and state assessments. It includes: language and literacy skills; study skills; and self-efficacy.

ADHD is an acronym for *attention deficit/hyperactivity disorder*. There are a variety of terms used to describe this disorder as the naming of it has changed with each successive publication of the Diagnostic Statistical Manual. Attention disorders are currently categorized into three subtypes: the inattentive type; the hyperactive type; and the combined type. A great deal of new research into the disorder indicates that ADHD involves executive function. See Thomas E. Brown's *A New Understanding of ADHD in Children and Adults: Executive Function Impairments* (2013) and Russell A. Barkley's Executive Functions: *What They Are, How They Work, and Why They Evolved* (2012) for deeper understanding of the complexities of ADHD.

ANXIETY can manifest behaviorally in a variety of ways including: task avoidance, irritability, emotional outbursts, diminished or excessive activity, somatization (i.e., feelings of pain or illness that seem to have no physical cause), and dissociation (e.g., "spacing out," day dreaming, etc.). Even minor levels of anxiety can profoundly disrupt the learning process.

ATTENTION references the brain's skill at identifying relevant incoming sensory information in order to initiate and maintain focus for a defined period of time, and shift that focus as necessary.

AUTOMATICITY is the ability to perform a task quickly and accurately with little or no conscious effort. In terms of reading, automaticity refers to immediate word recognition with no need to sound out the word phonetically.

DECLARATIVE MEMORY (EPISODIC AND SEMANTIC MEMORY) is our own unique body of knowledge. It consists of episodic memory and semantic memory. Episodic memory is knowledge (including emotions) gained through our personal life experiences. Semantic memory is our factual and conceptual knowledge base—the sum of what we know about the world from both direct personal experience and indirect experience (e.g., book learning).

DIAGNOSTIC ASSESSMENT is a category of assessment. Its purpose is to determine what difficulties a student is having and why. It can be formal (as in the tools used during neuropsychological, educational, speech-language, or behavioral evaluations) or informal (as in well-designed classroom assessments).

EDUCATIONAL EVALUATION refers to a series of diagnostic assessments and interviews with teachers, parents, and the student. Its purpose is to determine: what difficulties a student is experiencing; why; whether those difficulties are the result of a learning or other disability; and what educational interventions should be implemented to remediate the difficulties. An educational evaluation is similar to a neuropsychological evaluation, but is generally shorter in duration, assesses fewer areas of functioning, and is commonly carried out by a team that includes a psychologist, special education teacher(s), and other school specialists as needed.

EFFORT refers to the energy we expend to carry out an action. Effort is expended in intensity and duration. After our sensory, memory, and motivational systems are involved, our brains arouse us to exert effort.

EXECUTIVE FUNCTION is the coordination of cognitive and psychological processes that enable an individual to set goals, carry out a plan that achieves those goals, and self-monitor and shift approaches as needed.

EXPLICIT INSTRUCTION is a systematic approach to instruction that includes very high levels of teacher and student interaction and instructional principles that guide how content is selected and delivered. These principles include providing students with the big picture and purpose of the work; eliciting students' background knowledge; clear modeling, practicing of specific strategies and sharing feedback; scaffolding; guiding students' application of knowledge and strategies in varying contexts; and frequent individualized reviewing of material to ensure that previously learned content and strategies are retained, used, and built upon.

INTERNAL LANGUAGE refers to self-talk and self-questioning. All individuals use internal language to mediate sensory input. It is an essential component of executive function, as well as being important to self-efficacy and the comprehension and production of language. For example, people use internal language to motivate themselves when they're discouraged: "I know I can do this because I did it last week!" They use it to calm themselves: "I'm feeling sick because I'm nervous about my math test. I know if I breathe slowly and do the work carefully I'll be just fine." They use it to manage comprehension: "The teacher just said there were two villains in the story, but I only remember one. I need to go back and look at the story or ask the teacher about this."

LANGUAGE AND LITERACY SKILLS are terms used together in this book to underscore that listening and speaking skills provide the foundation for developing reading and writing skills. Often, schools use *literacy skills* in reference to reading and writing only. *Content literacy* and *disciplinary literacy* refer to understanding and using the vocabulary and patterns of thinking related to a specific academic discipline such as mathematics or history. *Language and literacy skills* are those required to comprehend and produce language including listening, speaking, reading, and writing.

LANGUAGE-BASED TEACHING / INSTRUCTION is individualized or classroom instruction with the specific purpose of remediating or developing language and literacy skills.

LEARNING DIFFERENCE All students who seem to have more potential than their school performance indicates—whether or not they meet diagnostic criteria for a learning disorder/disability—exhibit a learning difference. They adapt less effectively or independently than others in learning situations that do not match their learning style, regardless of their effort. They do not learn the material as well, and their performance falls below their potential. Their learning difference can create a cycle of anxiety, frustration, and reduced self-esteem that makes it even more difficult to learn.

LEARNING DISABILITY People with a learning disability have been diagnosed with or meet the diagnostic criteria for a specific learning disorder according to the *Diagnostic and Statistical Manual of Mental Disorders*, the American Psychiatric Association (APA) publication that guides physicians' and neuropsychologists' diagnoses. Individuals with a language-based learning disability (LBLD) are those whose difficulties specifically relate to the ways they perceive, process, and produce language (listening, speaking, reading, and writing). From a neuropsychological point of view, a specific learning disorder (called specific learning disability in educational circles) describes individuals whose brains function so differently from most others that even though they have average-to-superior cognitive capacities, they cannot learn *the same way* most people do.

LEARNING STYLE refers to a student's individual preferences for absorbing and expressing information and ideas. It is the set of preferences each of us brings to a learning experience. In most cases learning style is distinct from "learning difference" and "learning disability," which are both terms used to indicate interferences to optimum informational and emotional processing, and demonstration of learning.

LONG-TERM MEMORY allows us to hold information over extended periods—sometimes a lifetime. Contrary to the image many people have of long-term memory as a vast collection of archived data, most of our memories are actually reconstructions. They are not stored in our brains like books on library shelves. Actually, when we remember something, we reconstruct it from elements scattered throughout our brains. Long-term memory consists of two systems: declarative memory and procedural memory.

MEMORY is the brain's skill at acquiring, storing, and accessing information. How memory works is the object of enthusiastic enquiry. Memory and learning are different, but they depend on each other. Learning is a modification that happens when the brain absorbs new information and associates it with information stored in memory. Memory is the brain's ability to reconstruct what it has stored and reclassify it using new information.

MOTIVATION In an overview of motivational theories, Richard W. Scholl, a professor of organizational behavior at the University of Rhode Island

(2002) proposes that motivation is what energizes, directs, and sustains our behavior. It dictates how much effort we put into action, what makes us choose one course of action over another, and what influences how long we persevere in the action. Motivation can be internal or external. Internal motivation refers to the desire to do something because it gives us pleasure or helps us develop into the kind of person we want to be. External motivation refers to the desire to engage in behavior because it leads to an external reward that we desire.

NEUROBIOLOGICAL DIFFERENCES are differences in the way an individual's brain processes stimulation, including language.

NEUROPSYCHOLOGICAL EVALUATION refers to a series of diagnostic assessments and interviews with teachers, parents, and the student. Its purpose is to determine: what difficulties a student is experiencing; why; whether those difficulties are the result of a learning or other disability; and what educational interventions should be implemented to remediate the difficulties. A neuropsychological evaluation is similar to an educational evaluation, but assesses more cognitive and psychological areas of functioning, and is carried out by a neuropsychologist with input from as many individuals who work with the student as possible.

PROCEDURAL MEMORY Unlike declarative memory which requires conscious reconstruction, procedural memory seems unconscious. Actions guided by our procedural memory are automatic (including conditioned emotional responses). The automaticity results from the constant repetition of a motor or cognitive task. For example, most people tie their shoes or chew their food with seemingly no conscious thought. Their procedural memory for these tasks developed as a result of explicit instruction and practice provided by their caregivers over time.

SELF-ADVOCACY is the assertion or negotiation of one's interests, needs, and rights.

SELF-ASSESSMENT has two definitions. First, it is the evaluation of one's strengths and weaknesses in any given area. In addition, it refers to a form of classroom assessment in which students evaluate their own work according to a given set of criteria.

SELF-AWARENESS is the cognizance of one's own personality and character traits, unique strengths and weaknesses, feelings, and behaviors.

SELF-EFFICACY is the belief that one's actions are related to outcomes. A person who connects actions to positive outcomes will say, "I practice soccer every day. That helped me make the team," instead of, "I guess I got lucky." A person who connects actions to negative outcomes will say, "I forgot to bring my book home last night, so I couldn't read. That's why I failed the quiz today," not, "Those questions were too specific. The quiz was totally unfair." The idea of self-efficacy lies at the center of Albert Bandura's social-cognitive theory.

SENSORY PROCESSING DISORDER Some people are able to perceive sensory input but may process it differently from others. Sensory processing disorder (also referred to as sensory integration disorder) is a term used to describe the difficulties of individuals whose sensory systems do not organize sensory input into appropriate motor and/or behavioral responses. As a result, these individuals may experience physical discomfort or even danger, emotional distress, and social and academic difficulties. While commonly seen on evaluations of students with school difficulties, sensory processing disorder is not a diagnostic category in the American Psychiatric Association's *Diagnostic Statistic Manual of Mental Disorders* (DSM-V). The APA's editorial group determined that more research is required to determine whether interferences with sensory processing constitute a distinct disorder, or are a feature of other disorders.

SHORT-TERM AND INTERMEDIATE-TERM MEMORY allow us to hold small bits of information for short periods of time—seconds to minutes. Both have limited capacity, but can be extended by chunking bits together. Short- and intermediate-term memory are terms sometimes used interchangeably with working memory capacity.

SKILLS AND STRATEGIES are terms often used interchangeably, but they are actually different. A *strategy* is one specific approach to achieve a goal. For example, summarizing a chapter after reading is one strategy to aid in retention of the content. Other strategies may include highlighting, taking margin notes, making an outline, answering the questions at the end of the chapter, and creating index cards for vocabulary. A *skill* is the flexible and successful use of one or a combination of appropriate strategies in order to achieve a goal.

STUDY SKILLS is a term that refers to an array of organizational, learning, and memory strategies that empower individuals to manage materials, time, and language.

WORKING MEMORY is closely linked to attention. Working memory allows us to hold different bits of information in mind in order to do something with them. Working memory capacity is the number of separate pieces of information an individual can hold in mind (e.g., the numbers and signs in an arithmetic problem). Working memory capability refers to how we organize and manipulate this information (e.g., solving the arithmetic problem). Cowan defines working memory capability as "how well attention can be used to keep a task goal active in the presence of interference" (2005, p. viii).

NOTES

Recommended Resources

Executive Function

Executive Functions: What They Are, How They Work, and Why They Evolved (2012)
Russell A. Barkley

A New Understanding of ADHD in Children and Adults: Executive Function Impairments (2013)
Thomas E. Brown

Coaching Students with Executive Skills Deficits (2012)
Peg Dawson and Richard Guare

Executive Skills in Children and Adolescents, 2nd edition (2010)
Peg Dawson and Richard Guare

Assessment and Intervention for Executive Function Difficulties (2009)
George McCloskey, Lisa A. Perkins, & Bob Van Divner

Executive Function in Education: From Theory to Practice (2007)
Lynn Meltzer, editor

Promoting Executive Function in the Classroom (2010)
Lynn Meltzer

Executive Function 101 (2013 ebook)
National Center for Learning Disabilities

Emotional Processing

Smart but Stuck: Emotions in Teens and Adults with ADHD (2014)
Thomas E. Brown

Emotional Intelligence: Why It Can Matter More Than IQ (2005)
Daniel Goleman

Mindfulness for Beginners: Reclaiming the Present Moment—and Your Life
(2011)
Jon Kabat-Zinn

Trauma Through a Child's Eyes: Awakening the Ordinary Miracle of Healing
(2006)
Peter A. Levine

*A Still Quiet Place: A Mindfulness Program for Teaching Children and
Adolescents to Ease Stress and Difficult Emotions* (2014)
Amy Saltzman

The Body Keeps the Score: Brain, Mind, and Body in the Healing of Trauma
(2014)
Bessel Van der Kolk

Learning and Teaching

Frames of Mind: The Theory of Multiple Intelligences (2011)
Howard Gardner

On Being A Teacher (2009)
Jonathan Kozol

The Courage to Teach (2007)
Parker J. Palmer

The Skillful Teacher (2008)
Jon Saphier, Mary Ann Haley-Speca, Robert Gower

Thinking Styles (2007)
Robert J. Sternberg

Teaching for Wisdom, Intelligence, Creativity, and Success (2009)
Robert J. Sternberg, Linda Jarvin, & Elena L. Grigorenko

Teaching for Successful Intelligence: To Increase Student Learning and Achievement (2007)
Robert J. Sternberg and Elena L. Grigorenko

From The Landmark School Outreach Program

Language-Based Teaching Series

Executive Function and Foundations for Learning and Teaching (2014)
Patricia W. Newhall

Language-Based Learning Disabilities (2012)
Patricia W. Newhall

Landmark School Teaching Guides

From Talking to Writing: Strategies for Scaffolding Expository Expression (2002)
Terrill M. Jennings and Charles W. Haynes

Multiplication and Division Facts for the Whole-to-Part, Visual Learner (2013)
Christopher J. Woodin

Study Skills: Reasearch-Based Teaching Strategies (2008)
Patricia W. Newhall

Teaching Independent Minds (2008)
Patricia W. Newhall

Thinking About Language: Helping Students Say What They Mean and Mean What They Say (2003)
Roberta Stacey

Writing (1995)
Jean Tarricone

Understanding Language-Based Learning Disabilities Series

Difficulties with Mathematics
Kathleen M. Hamon

Making Sense of Language-Based Learning Disabilities
Patricia W. Newhall

Receptive and Expressive Language Disorders
Melody O'Neil

Social Communication Skills
Linda Gross

Study Skills and Academic Competence
Patricia W. Newhall

Writing Research Papers
Erin Broudo

References

American Psychiatric Association. (2000). Diagnostic and statistical manual of mental disorders (text revision). Washington, DC: Author.

Anderson, V., Jacobs, R., & Anderson, P. J. (Eds.) (2008). Executive functions and the frontal lobes: A lifespan perspective. New York: Taylor & Francis.

Barkley, R. A. (1997). ADHD and the nature of self-control. New York: Guilford Press.

Barkley, R. A. (2012). Executive functions: *What they are, how they work, and why they evolved.* New York: Guilford Press.

Bradley, M. M. (2000). Emotion and motivation. In J. T. Cacioppo, L. G. Tassinary, & G. G. Berntson (Eds.), Handbook of psychophysiology (2nd ed., pp. 602-642). New York: Cambridge University Press.

Brown, T. E. (2005). Attention deficit disorder: The unfocused mind in children and adults. New Haven, CT: Yale University Press.

Brown, T. E. (2007). A new approach to attention deficit disorder. Educational Leadership 64, 22-27.

Brown, T. E. (2013, July 5) DSM-5 changes in ADHD diagnostic criteria. Retrieved November 25, 2013, from http://www.drthomasebrown.com/dsm-5-changes-in-adhd-diagnostic-criteria/).

Connor, D. J. (2005). Studying disability and disability studies: Shifting paradigms of LD – A synthesis of responses to Reid and Valle. Journal of Learning Disabilities, 38(2), 159-174.

Cowan, N. (2005). Working memory capacity. New York: Psychology Press.

D'Andrea, W., Ford, F., Stolbach, B., Spinazzola, J. & van der Kolk, B. (2012). Understanding interpersonal trauma in children: Why we need a developmentally appropriate trauma diagnosis. *American Journal of Orthopsychiatry* 82(2), 187-200.

Dawson, P., & Guare, R. (2010). Executive skills in children and adolescents: A practical guide to assessment and intervention. New York: Guilford Press.

Dudley-Marling, C. (2004, November). The social construction of learning disabilities. Journal of Learning Disabilities, 37(6), 482-489. Retrieved March 30, 2008, from Professional Development Collection database.

Durlak, J. A., Weissberg, R. P., Dymnicki, A. B., Taylor, R. D., & Schellinger, K. B. (2011). The impact of enhancing students' social and emotional learning: A meta-analysis of school-based universal interventions. Child Development 82(1), 405-432.

Fisher, D., and Fry, N. (2008). *Better learning through structured teaching: A framework for the gradual release of responsibility, 2nd edition.* Alexandria, VA: ASCD.

Foucault, M. (1972). The archaeology of knowledge and the discourse on language. New York: Pantheon.

Gardner, H. (1983). Frames of mind: The theory of multiple intelligences. New York: Basic Books.

Gardner, H. (2007). Hill, skill and will: Executive function from a multiple intelligences perspective. In L. Meltzer (Ed.), *Executive function in education: From theory to practice*. New York: Guilford Press.

Gardner, H. (2006). Multiple intelligences: New horizons. New York: Basic Books.

Goleman, D. (1995). *Emotional intelligence: Why it can matter more than IQ*. New York: Bantam.

Hsieh, P., Sullivan, J. R., & Guerra, N. S. (2007). A closer look at college students: Self-efficacy and goal orientation. *Journal of Advanced Academics*, 18(3), 454-476.

Huitt, W. (2011). Motivation to learn: An overview. Educational Psychology Interactive. Valdosta, GA: Valdosta State University. Retrieved 6/5/13 from http://www.edpsycinteractive.org/topics/motivation/motivate.html

Koltko-Rivera, M.E. (2006). Rediscovering the later version of Maslow's hierarchy of needs: Self-transcendence and opportunities for theory, research, and unification. *Review of general psychology*. 10 (4): 302-317.

Kabat-Zinn, J. (2012). *Mindfulness for beginners*. Boulder, CO: Sounds True, Inc.

Lavoie, R. (2007). *The motivation breakthrough: 6 secrets to turning on the tuned-out child*. New York: Touchstone.

Lewis, P.A., Critchley, H.D., Rotshtein, P., & Dolan, J. (2007). Neural correlates of processing valence and arousal in affective words. *Cerebral cor-*

tex. 17 (3): 742-748.

Mascolo, M. (2014). I used to be such a good teacher—until I started holding myself accountable. Pedagogy and the Human Sciences, https://www.linkedin.com/groups/Pedagogy-Human-Sciences-3699669

Maslow, A. (1943). A theory of human motivation. Psychological Review, 50, 370-396. Retrieved 6/613 from http://psychclassics.yorku.ca/Maslow/motivation.htm.

Maslow, A. (1971). The farther reaches of human nature. New York: The Viking Press.

McCloskey, G., Perkins, L. A., & Van Divner, B. (2009). Assessment and intervention for executive function difficulties. New York: Routledge.

Meltzer, L. (2010). Promoting executive function in the classroom. New York: Guilford Press.

Merton, R. C. (1968). The Matthew effect in science. Science 159(3810), 56-63, www.garfieldlibrary.upenn.edu/merton/matthew1.pdf

Mooney, J., & Cole, D. (2000). Learning outside the lines: Two Ivy League students with learning disabilities and ADHD give you the tools. New York: Fireside.

Neuroscience Research Center (NRC). (1994). Learning and memory. Retrieved July 21, 2011, from The University of Texas Health Science Center at Houston Web site: http://nba.uth.tmc.edu/nrc/content/research/learning-and-memory.htm

Ochsner, K. N., & Phelps, E. (2007). Emerging perspectives on emotion-cognition interactions. TRENDS in Cognitive Science 11(8), 317-318.

Reid, D. K., & Valle, J. W. (2004). The discursive practice of learning disability: Implications for instruction and parent-school relations. Journal of Learning Disabilities, 37(6), 466-481.

Scholl, R. W. (2002). What is motivation? Retrieved May 30, 2013, from the Charles T. Schmidet Labor Research Center at University of Rhode Island Web site: http://www.uri.edu/research/lrc/scholl/webnotes/Motivation.htm

Sternberg, R. J. (1997). Thinking styles. New York: Cambridge University Press.

Sternberg, R. J. (2007). Wisdom, intelligence, and creativity synthesized. New York: Cambridge University Press.

Yuen, E. Y., Wei, J., Zhong, W. L. P., Li, X., and Yan, Z. (8 March 2012). *Neuron*. Repeated stress causes cognitive impairment by suppressing glutamate receptor expression and function in prefrontal cortex. 73(5), 962-977.

NOTES

Acknowledgments

This book is the result of Landmark Outreach's ongoing efforts to empower students through their teachers. It could not have been produced without the dedication and support of many people. I'd like to express my deep appreciation to Dan Ahearn, Director of Landmark School Outreach Program, for his unwavering commitment to putting practical information and strategies into teachers' hands, and his patience and support through the multiple revisions and delays in the production of this second book in the *Language-Based Teaching Series*. In addition to acknowledging them, I'd also like to express admiration for the teachers at Landmark School whose tireless and committed efforts to empower their students' learning have transformed so many lives through the years. The pedagogy that has continued to develop since Landmark School's founding in 1971 is reflected in Landmark Outreach's consulting, courses, and publications.

Thank you to Dottie Seiter and Liz Sweibel for their editorial guidance; to John Hall of *johnhalldesign.com* for the cover design; to my Outreach colleagues, Dan Ahearn, Kathryn Frye, Keryn Kwedor, and Kaitlin Loughlin for their copyediting efforts; and to my students (youngsters *and* adults) who continue to teach me how to be a better teacher.

I'd like to acknowledge my husband, Charles L. Newhall, an inspired teacher, for twenty years of passionate discussions about teaching and learning and psychology that have helped shape my thinking about the work we do in classrooms and schools. Finally, I thank my children, John and Sarah, and their friends and friends' parents, whose stories about their struggles and successes with school continue to motivate me to teach and write about education.

LANDMARK OUTREACH PUBLICATIONS

Landmark Outreach publications model evidence-based practical strategies that develop students' listening, speaking, reading, and writing skills. They provide the guidance and materials you need to enhance language-based instruction.

Join our mailing list and receive a **FREE** subscription to our e-resource, *Spotlight on Language-Based Teaching*! View archived issues on our website, www.landmarkoutreach.org.

While you're online, investigate our other books and booklets on language-based teaching. You can read about the authors and view sample pages of our materials.

LEARN MORE!
LANDMARK OUTREACH PROFESSIONAL DEVELOPMENT
CONSULTING
SUMMER PROFESSIONAL DEVELOPMENT INSTITUTES
ONLINE LEARNING

WWW.LANDMARKOUTREACH.ORG

About the Author

Patricia W. Newhall, M.A., M.S. Ed., is Associate Director of the Landmark School Outreach Program. A teacher of literature, writing, and study skills since 1987, she has taught at the middle school, high school, college and post-graduate levels, and has worked in public and independent schools. In her publications, lectures, and graduate courses, she shares research about learning disabilities and differences, and the teaching strategies essential to building the skills and confidence of struggling learners. Newhall is the author of a variety of magazine and online articles, as well as several Landmark Outreach publications including *Language-Based Learning Disabilities*; *Study Skills: Research-Based Teaching Strategies*; and *Teaching Independent Minds* She welcomes communication from fellow educators and parents of struggling learners. Please feel free to contact her by posting comments and questions on this book's homepage at www.landmarkoutreach.org/publications.

NOTES